Mountain Biking
— in the —
SCOTTISH
HIGHLANDS

D1427996

AUTHOR'S NOTE

The success of this little book has encouraged me to produce another one, called simply

Mountain Biking in the Scottish Highlands – Volume 2

obtainable in all good bookshops. I should like to emphasize that the tours described in Volume 2 are quite different to those in this book.

Mountain Biking
— in the —
SCOTTISH HIGHLANDS

FRANCES FLEMING

𝓗H

Alexander Heriot

Alexander Heriot & Co. Ltd.
P.O. Box 1, Northleach
Cheltenham, Gloucestershire

British Library Cataloguing in Publication Data
Fleming, Frances, 1955 —
  Mountain Biking in the Scottish Highlands.
  1. Mountainous regions. Cycling
  I. Title
  796.609143

ISBN 0-906382-07-6

First published 1990
Reprinted 1992
© 1990 text and maps D. F. Fleming

Design and production Colin Reed and Peter Loveday
Typeset by Gilcott Graphics, Rushden, Northants.
Printed and bound in Great Britain by
Woolnough Bookbinding Ltd., Irthlingborough, Northants.

Contents

Maps

A general map of Scotland is on page viii

Each route has its own area map and contour profile

Three-cabled bridge in Glen Nevis

Acknowledgements

I would like to thank the following people for their invaluable assistance: Philip Bowden-Smith, Tim and Helen Healy, Alasdair Ross, Jan and Willie Orr, Graham Moncur and Mike Futty. Special thanks to Adrian Van Herwynen, who is responsible for the Inverary tour, and whose biking knowledge helped this book from fantasy to reality.

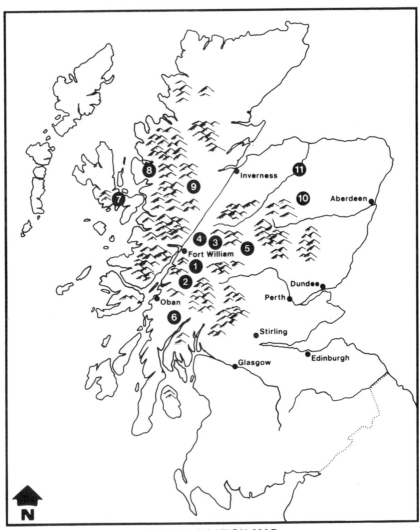

ROUTE LOCATION MAP

Introduction

Scotland in general and the Highlands in particular offer some of the finest mountain biking country imaginable. The hills and glens provide pleasures and challenges in such profusion and of such variety that it is difficult to decide which are the 'best' routes. Some of you may prefer the soaring peaks of the Cuillins on the Isle of Skye, others the rolling heather-clad moors of the east and for some just weaving from distillery to distillery along the whisky tour of Speyside will suffice.

This guide aims to have something for everyone, whether you are a go-it-alone dedicated enthusiast, a holiday group, family or pensioner. There are tours of different length, of different grades of difficulty and of varying ratios of track to tarmac so that everyone of whatever age or ability, from couch potato to Olympic aspirant, will find something to their taste.

Most of this book is self-explanatory but there are some background aspects to bicycling in Scotland, as distinct from other countries, of which overseas visitors may have little or no knowledge and these deserve a mention.

Public Access

There is, in Scotland, no automatic right of access over someone else's land. You must either have the owner's permission to be on his land or you must use a 'public right of way' (see below). And even though the land looks completely desolate and unpopulated, it will always have an owner, whether it is a private individual, the Forestry Commission, the National Trust or whoever. There is no specific penalty for trespass, since damage or nuisance must first be proved, but it is within the legal rights of an owner or his representative to remove any trespasser who declines to leave voluntarily.

So much for the theory. In practice, however, there exists in Scotland a long tradition of consideration and co-operation between landowners and walkers and permission is seldom refused for sensible land use so long as it does not interfere with other activities (see Periods of Restricted Access, below). If, therefore, you intend to leave the public right of way, it is worth making the effort to find someone who can give you the necessary permission. Not only is it an act of courtesy but also one of commonsense since landowners and their employees invariably know useful things like how far the next shop is, who has the best B&B in the area, whether a river is fordable, which footbridge has been swept away in the winter and so on. Moreover, landowners provide, free of charge, much of the bothy accommodation (see below) that you may wish to use. So it makes sense and costs nothing to ask permission before camping or leaving the beaten track.

All the tours in this book are on trails and tracks which are public rights of way. These have their roots in history and have developed from the days before the invention of the motor car and the subsequent growth of the present road system. As all journeys were then necessarily made on foot or horseback or by horse-drawn vehicles, traditional cross-country routes became established — old drove roads, military roads, Kirk roads, estate roads — for regular use by the public. Most rights of way are clearly marked on the Ordnance Survey maps. It must also be mentioned that because bicycling involves muscle rather than engine power, so bicyclists have the same legal entitlements on public rights of way as do walkers. But this must not be abused. Walkers very understandably resent bikers who force them off the path or otherwise behave selfishly — and at the moment there are more walkers than bikers!

Part of the attraction of these wild and remote places is the lack of any evidence that another human being was there before you, so if you are intending to camp on any of these tours, please use your commonsense; *do not* light your fire in the middle of a smooth green sward but find somewhere else i.e. a gravel patch or beach where remains can easily be buried or destroyed. By the same token *do not* leave your sardine tins or empty crisp packets around — take your rubbish with you.

Fire

You may find it hard to believe in a country famous for its rainfall, but fire is one of the greatest hazards in Scotland. The most dangerous time is between March and June when the new season's growth has yet to emerge and the ground is covered in piles of long, dry, dead grass from winter. An ill-considered camp-fire, a burning match, even a casually thrown cigarette-end − any of these can, in a few moments, start a blaze that will eventually cover hundreds of acres and destroy not only the natural flora but also the nests, eggs or chicks of ground-nesting birds. Trees are especially vulnerable to fire: what little natural woodland remains in Scotland has a tough enough existence already with grazing animals and harsh weather conditions contributing to make its life a fragile one.

A simple rhyme to remember at all time −

That which burns
never returns.

Follow the Code

An easy code to follow is the Off-Road Code issued by the Mountain Bike Club:

- Only ride where you have the legal right
- Always yield to horses and pedestrians
- Avoid animals and crops wherever possible
- Take all litter with you
- Leave all gates as found
- Never create a fire hazard
- Keep unnecessary noise to a minimum
- Always try to be self-sufficient for you and your bike.

Periods of Restricted Access

There are times when it is imperative to get permission locally before leaving a public right of way. These are:

- The lambing season (mainly April and May).
- The grouse shooting season (from the 12th August through September).
- The deer stalking season (normally August to mid-October).

Remember that you are on holiday but that others have to earn their living from the countryside. If you insist on biking through a flock of sheep that a man has spent the whole day 'gathering' in the surrounding hills, do not be surprised if you get an unfriendly reception when you meet him and his dogs.

Best Times

The best months for bicycling in Scotland are May and June − the summer rains have yet to start and the midges are still in hiding. Nevertheless waterproofs should be carried at *all times* (see below) and midge repellent should not be eschewed during the midge season — approximately July, August and September.

Many of the tours necessitate fording rivers and burns which can rise and fall very rapidly, a gentle crossing becoming an impassable torrent in a short time — plan accordingly.

Because of the distance between shops, early closing and Sunday observance, it is always advisable to carry some food — and watch your petrol if you are travelling by car.

The Bike

A sturdy well-maintained mountain bike is essential for the tours in this guide — it will be subject to copious amounts of water, mud, rocks and peat, often all at once.

Since all of these tours involve some amount of tarmac riding, you might consider a combination tyre. These have knobs for traction as well as a centre head for quieter performance and lower friction on tarmac. Most tyre-manufacturers make such a tyre — consult a bike shop for details. Whichever one you choose, remember that the fatter the tyre the less likely you are to sink in a peat bog. A width of 1.9″ (4.75 cm) seems to be a good compromise, rolling well on tarmac yet providing good off-road performance.

A comfortable saddle is a must: few things can make a ride more miserable than saddle sores. While there are many styles of seats available, and choosing the right one for you is vital, it is far more important to spend time on your bike 'hardening' your body to the saddle.

While many say they are confining, toe-clips greatly enhance your performance on the bike and once you have become used to them, you will wonder how you ever rode without them. They are an inexpensive way to significantly upgrade your performance.

Brakes should be checked regularly and kept in close adjustment. If the going is wet and muddy, stop frequently to clean the grooves in the brake pads.

A working knowledge of the bike and basic emergency repair is imperative. The terrain these tours cover is very conducive to flat tyres, broken spokes, stuck chains etc., all of which are only a minor inconvenience to someone with tools and know-how but are a distinct disaster to anyone not so equipped. There are many bicycle repair manuals and bike shop professionals available to help you put together a small tool kit and to familiarise you with emergency repairs. Take the time to learn before heading off into the wilds; replacing an inner-tube during a rainstorm on a windswept moor is a far less distressing thought if you have practised it a few times over a pint in front of the fireplace – though mind you it's still a pretty distressing thought! In Scotland, bicycle shops with the parts and expertise required by today's hi-tech mountain bikes are few and far between (see page 106), and these tours can be hard on the bikes – be prepared.

Clothing

Due to the variability of Scotland's weather, which can change almost at the blink of an eye, it is wise to be prepared for anything that nature might throw at you, regardless of the forecast or how fine the morning may be.

Several light layers are better than one heavy one as you are better able to control your temperature by adding or removing clothes. The outermost layer should be a waterproof of some kind (preferably a breathable fabric, expensive but worth it), and all layers should allow plenty of movement and be comfortable.

Padded cycling shorts are a must for such long distances: they are extremely comfortable and will save wear and tear on your bum. Likewise a pair of padded cycling gloves will make riding (and falling) more comfortable and will help prevent the numbness many mountain bikers experience after long hard rides.

While bicycle touring shoes are good, any comfortable pair of trainers or tennis shoes will do as well. It is important that they do not fit too loosely as blisters can result.

Whether or not you wear a helmet is a personal decision – the terrain is difficult, help can be a long time coming and falling down is easy – the choice is yours.

Since many of the directions in the Route Logs necessarily refer to points of the compass, it is highly advisable to include one in your kit. This may seem a needless precaution on a fine and cloudless day but anyone who has been caught in the hills by the sudden descent of an impenetrable layer of mist will know how easy it is to completely lose one's bearings.

Bothies

In several of the remote mountain areas in Scotland, you will come across what appear to be abandoned cottages. These are bothies which are left open for the use of passers-by. They belong to and are made available by the estate on whose land they are situated. Many are in the care of the Mountain Bothies Association, a voluntary working association whose stated object is 'to maintain simple unlocked shelters in remote areas'. You are therefore requested to be careful in their use since misuse can lead to the loss of a valued facility. The quality of bothies is variable and depends on the level of maintenance, popularity and most importantly the habits of those who use them. Those relevant to these tours range from pretty squalid to immaculate. If you are seriously depending on them as part of your itinerary it would be wise to check with the estate concerned that they are still in use. A list of appropriate telephone numbers is on page 110. Be warned that during the holiday season and weekends some of the more popular ones can become extremely crowded.

About this Guide

I have attempted to begin and end each tour at the same place. Where this was not possible the routes begin and end at railway stations. The mileages (km) indicated in the logs are based on cycle computers and will vary in some cases from your own mileages because of such factors as weight difference, tyre pressure and those times you have to shoulder the load.

The maps and profiles provided have been specifically designed to be used in conjunction with the Ordnance Survey (OS) Landranger maps listed at the beginning of each tour and *not* by themselves. Much of Scotland is vast and remote and the weather can change suddenly and dramatically: it would be foolish and dangerous not to consult the appropriate maps regularly.

Scotland is a country as yet largely unspoilt by the hand of man and if it is to remain this way, the mountains and glens, which owing to their very remoteness are mostly tourist free, must be treated with the greatest respect. Mountain biking in America is causing one of the most divisive storms to blow through the national conservation movement in recent memory. In parks near San Francisco, Rangers have been forced to close routes, set up speed-traps and use radar guns to curb the fast and reckless riding which is causing erosion and damage to the landscape and driving hikers and equestrians from trails. Bikers in the US reply that their sport is an efficient, safe, fitness-promoting way to get back to nature and that it rarely interferes with the pleasures of others. Nevertheless their burgeoning numbers have caused safety and ecological concerns and prompted pleas from all over the country to ban them. This may seem a far cry from Scotland but in Britain and the rest of Europe mountain biking is on the increase and we ignore what is happening in America at our peril.

It is ironic that it is our love for the mountains and remote tracks and trails that may also spoil them. Simple actions can make all the difference − never skid or lock your wheels when braking and avoid riding across ground which is easily eroded i.e. scree, bogs etc. If our behaviour to the environment and to the people who live and work in it is considerate at all times then we shall be responsible for helping keep intact the romance and integrity of Scotland's remarkable landscape.

Fort William Tours

Area information

Fort William today is a Mecca for climbers, hillwalkers and mountain bikers. Situated on the shores of Loch Linnhe and with Ben Nevis, the tallest mountain in Great Britain, a mere four miles away, it is a sightseer's and photogapher's paradise.

The fort after which this town is named was built in 1655 and enlarged in 1690. It was named after William III. Nothing now remains of the actual fort which was dismantled in 1860 and demolished in 1890 to provide space for the railway and station. There are numerous restaurants and tourist shops in the town and accommodation to suit any taste. An excellent tourist information centre is located in the centre of town and the West Highland Museum houses an interesting collection of Jacobite relics along with local art and craft work. Fort William forms one end of the West Highland Way, the other end being at Milngavie 95 miles (152 km) to the south. Easily the most famous of Highland foot-paths, the West Highland Way (WHW) is used by approximately 70,000 people annually. The first long distance footpath to be established under the Countryside Act of 1967, it was officially opened in 1980. Many of the tracks, trails and drove roads used in the WHW follow ancient and historic routes. Extensive use is made of the military roads built in the 18th century by General Wade to help control Jacobite clansmen.

Fort William is probably most famous for its geographical association with Ben Nevis. The origin of the name Ben Nevis has caused much conjecture. It actually derives from the Gaelic Beinn-Neamh-Bhathais; Neamh meaning the heavens or clouds, Bhathais, the top of a man's head — the mountain with its head in the clouds. It is mostly seen from the south and west, giving the illusion of a shapeless lump — but its north side is the tallest and most splendid cliff in Britain. Many people climb Ben Nevis every year for the ascent is easy by the path up the back. On exceptionally fine days the coast of Ireland can just be seen a hundred and twenty miles away.

Glen Nevis links Fort William to Loch Treig by a pass of

twenty-two miles and gives access to more than forty mountain tops. Along its south flank, dividing it from Loch Leven, the Mamore range stretches seven miles in sixteen peaks; along the glen's north flank, dividing it from Glen Spean, sprawls the tallest mountain group in Britain — Ben Nevis, Carn Mor Dearg, Aonach Beag and Aonach Mor. The first three all exceed four thousand feet (1220 m) and the last falls only one foot under.

The River Nevis rises on Binnein Mor at the extreme eastern end of the Mamores and flows at first through desolate moorland at one thousand feet above sea level. Below Aonach Beag it enters a grassy strath and flows past the cottage at Steall. Here on the left a magnificent waterfall pours down the lowest cliff of Sgurr à Mhaim. It is 350 feet (106 m) high and one of the three biggest waterfalls in Scotland. The river then cuts through the bealloch* and drops four hundred feet down a gorge to Glen Nevis. The Nevis gorge is the finest example of its kind in Great Britain. It is four hundred feet high and the rocky walls are covered in pine, oak, birch and rowan trees. First the glaciers and then the water have forced their path around massive boulders, gouging great cauldrons and tunnels in the rock bed. It is a deep and tortuous channel and when in spate the gorge resounds to the water's thunder.

* A glossary of Scottish words will be found on p.111.

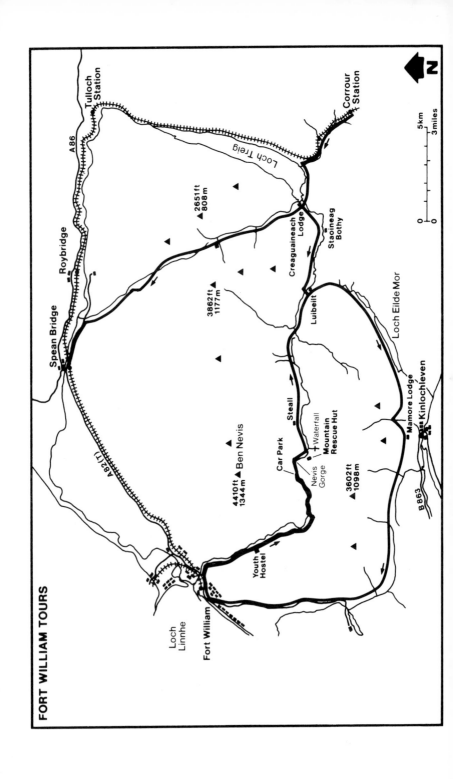

FORT WILLIAM TOURS

N

Corrour Station
Tulloch Station
A86
Loch Treig
Roybridge
2651ft 808m
Creaguaineach Lodge
Staoineag Bothy
Spean Bridge
3862ft 1177m
Luibeilt
Loch Eilde Mor
A82 (T)
Car Park
Steall
Waterfall
Mountain Rescue Hut
Mamore Lodge
Kinlochleven
4410ft 1344m ▲ Ben Nevis
Nevis Gorge
3602ft 1098m
B 863
Youth Hostel
Loch Linnhe
Fort William

0   5km
0   3miles

1

Fort William Loop
via Kinlochleven

Map: OS Landranger no. 41

Distance: 33.50 miles, 54.00 kilometres

Difficulty: challenging

Time: one day

Logistics: Train (Glasgow to Fort William) or car A82(T) to Fort William.

Route Description

21.45 miles (18.42km) trail; 12.05 miles (19.33km) tarmac.

This loop is interesting for the variety of riding conditions experienced in one day. From tarmac to unrideable trail, peat bog to hardpacked forestry track, vast open spaces to congested town riding, it is all here.

Leaving Fort William the route follows tarmac up Glen Nevis to a car park. From here the going gets rough and you will be carrying your bike for most of the next mile up a steep, narrow gorge. From the top of this, the trail to Luibeilt is rideable for most of its length, but watch out for the boggy bits. Once past Luibeilt it is generally good, passing Loch Eilde Beag and Loch Eilde Mor and climbing a short hill to the summit overlooking Loch Leven and the town of Kinlochleven. From this summit the track proceeds down a long (3.5 mile: 5.6km) incredibly fast descent. One of the best track speed downhills in this book (see also Corrour − Spean Bridge).

A short climb brings you to the junction with the West Highland Way, after which the track proceeds up a long glen, eventually connecting with tarmac at mile 28.30. From here into Fort William, the route follows the tarmac over a series of ups and downs, finishing with a one mile downhill through a residential area (many sidestreets; watch for children, dogs, cars etc). Follow the main street through Fort William back to the railway station.

With the exception of Mamore Lodge (or by making a detour into Kinlochleven), there are no facilities for food along this route once you leave Fort William. As this is a long one-day ride, plan accordingly.

This tour is a good, challenging work-out for the fit and experienced rider. Considering the difficulty of the terrain, the distance, and the miles between services, it is not a ride for the novice.

Route Log

00.00m (00.00km) Fort William railway station. All services available in the town, head north-east on the A82(T).

00.62 (01.00) Small roundabout, go straight over, signed to Glen Nevis and Glen Nevis youth hostel.

02.85 (04.00) Glen Nevis youth hostel.

06.85 (11.02) Carpark and the end of the tarmac. The next mile of trail is rocky, steep and almost entirely unrideable. Be prepared to carry your bike.

07.65 (12.30) Mountain Rescue club hut across three cable bridge on the right, near the base of the waterfall. Trail bears left.

08.20 (13.19) Ruin and bridge.

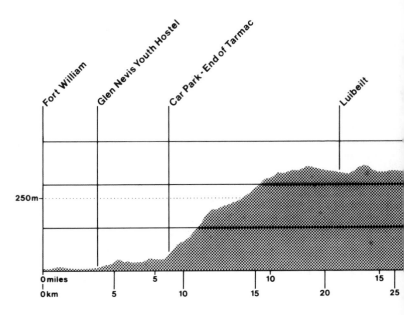

11.55 (18.60) Headwaters of the Water of Nevis, 1,319 feet (402m).

13.50 (21.72) Luibeilt, junction with trail to Corrour station and Spean Bridge: see tours on pages 29,33 and 41). The ruin here is dry, providing welcome relief from wind and rain. Follow obvious track heading south.

16.30 (26.22) Old bothy on the left. Messy but dry.

18.20 (29.28) Veer right where the track divides, begin climb.

18.70 (30.08) Summit, start of long steep descent.

20.80 (33.46) End of descent. Mamore Lodge, B&B, bar and snacks. Open all day. Begin climb.

21.60 (34.75) Summit.

22.00 (35.40) West Highland Way joins track.

24.40 (39.25) Summit and ruin.

28.20 (45.40) Keep left on track.

28.30 (45.53) Tarmac.

30.10 (48.43) Telephone.

31.95 (51.40) Summit and picnic area. Start of descent.

33.00 (53.00) Roundabout. Head right into the centre of Fort William.

33.50 (54.00) Fort William railway station.

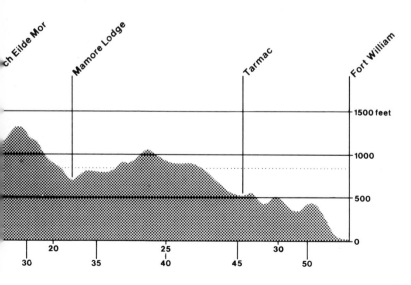

The Mamore Hills from the West Highland Way

2

Fort William – Taynuilt

Area information

Kinlochleven nestles at the foot of Mamore Forest, a range of mountains which totally dominate the landscape. The tour passes Mamore Lodge which perches six hundred feet above the village on the flank of Am Bodach (3,382ft: 1,031m), and must be one of the most splendidly sited houses in the West Highlands. It was formerly a shooting lodge, used by King Edward VII, and its site gives access to the deer-stalking tracks and disused roads that range to Glen Nevis, Loch Treig and Corrour, and Glen Spean (see Fort William and Corrour tours). Kinlochleven was built for the workers of the aluminium factory and hydro-electric power for the factory is supplied from the huge Blackwater reservoir four miles east in the hills behind Rannoch Moor. The dam for this reservoir was built in 1905 by a small army of workers encamped there. Many of these men died of cold and exposure when walking to and from the Kingshouse Hotel, the nearest public house, their bodies being discovered in the spring when the snow and ice melted.

This tour travels the same route as those men, between Beinn Bheag and Stob Mhic Martuin. It is the old military road built in 1750 by General Caulfield, is six miles long and drops steeply down to Glen Coe by way of the Devil's Staircase. As you descend the Staircase the imposing and craggy mountain before you is the Buachaille Etive Mór, 3,353 feet (1,022m) high. Its name means 'Great Shepherd' or 'Herdsman of Etive'. The rock is a rough rhyolite and is an extremely popular mountain with climbers.

To the right is the wild and imposing Glen Coe with its dark and mournful history, being the site of the massacre during the winter of 1691-2. This was a treacherous and bloody incident even by Scottish standards. The killers, payrolled by the English government and led by a Captain Campbell, had stayed in the glen for two weeks as guests of the Clan MacDonald before rising up in the night and murdering everyone. No mercy was shown; men, women and children were killed without distinction. Those that escaped the slaughter perished in the snow after Campbell and his men destroyed their homes.

The next stretch of this tour skirts the edge of Rannoch Moor. A thousand feet (330m) above sea level and covering an area of fifty-six square miles (14,745ha.), its rivers flow to both west and east coasts. The main drainage line of Rannoch is the River Bà, which falls from Clachlet to Loch Bà, Loch Laidon, Loch Rannoch and so to the Tummel and the Tay. There is a continuous line of river and loch stretching across the moor, and two unusual feats, swimming most of the way across in summer and skating across in winter, have actually been accomplished. At approximately mile twenty-seven of the tour you will have the magnificent Corrie Bà on your right. This gigantic corrie is the biggest in Scotland, exceeding in size even the famous Garbh Choire of Braeriach in the Cairngorms.

Corrie Bà is part of Blackmount, a forest returned to deer from sheep in 1820 by the Marquis of Breadalbane. The artist Landseer stayed here as a guest of the Breadalbane family and two of his major paintings, the Stag at Bay and the Deer Drive, were based on incidents that he witnessed at Blackmount. The Marchioness of Breadalbane was a formidable person, being one of the very few ladies of the nineteenth century who regularly took a rifle to the hill. She wore square-heeled boots and a voluminous ankle-length grey skirt which must have made hill-walking something of a feat in itself. She was also an inveterate gambler and in the 1930s the Breadalbanes were forced to sell Blackmount.

Splendid remnants of the vast Caledonian forest which formerly covered Scotland from Glen Coe to Braemar and from Glen Lyon to Glen Affric, can be found at Loch Tulla. This forest at one time harboured brown bears, wild boar, wolves and brigands. Its destruction by fire and felling occurred in two main phases, first between the ninth and twelfth centuries, when invading Vikings and warring clans set the woods alight to cover retreat and to halt or destroy enemies, and when they cut them for ship timbers. The second phase was between the fifteenth and eighteenth centuries when the English and Scots needed timber for iron smelting, the Highlanders were burning and felling to kill wolves and brigands and army commanders were doing the same to flush out rebels. The more recent needs of two World Wars have almost completed the destruction.

Dalmally is a good place to stop if you wish to break the tour into two days. The village stands on the old military road from Oban to Dumbarton and is in the heart of Campbell country. A short, single track tarmac ride will take you to Duncan Ban MacIntyre's monument; he was Scotland's most famous Gaelic poet (1722-1812) and the monument stands where, in Duncan's lifetime, the men of the township gathered twice yearly to hold their parliaments to decide how land should be farmed and to debate local problems. The view from this spot is superb. The church is also worth visiting. It is the third one to be built on this site and was completed in 1811 by the fourth Earl of Breadalbane. The churchyard has a fine collection of pre-reformation grave slabs, many of which mark the resting places of the MacGregors of Glen Strae, the Campbells of Glen Orchy, MacIntyres of Glen Noe and MacNabs of Barachasttain, all of whom at various times played an important part in the history of Loch Aweside.

Perhaps the best known of these are the MacGregors of Glen Strae whose name, like the MacDonalds of Glen Coe, is forever linked with tragedy. They were dispossessed by the Clan Campbell and forced to live as outlaws, first by 'Grey' Colin Campbell and later by his son, known as Black Duncan. The MacGregors eventually admitted defeat in 1611 when their stronghold, Glen Strae Castle, was destroyed.

Kilchurn Castle, 2 miles N.W. of Dalmally, was the home of the Campbells of Glen Orchy during this bloodthirsty period. The original tower was thought to have been built around 1450 by the wife of Colin Campbell while he was away on a Crusade. Sections were added later but the castle's importance to the Breadalbane family waned as their holdings to the east, in Perthshire, increased – they also owned castles Finlarig, Balloch and Taymouth. The roof of Kilchurn was removed around 1770 by a factor of the estate and used to rebuild Dalmally church and manse. Left open to the elements, it fell into ruin. Recently the Department of the Environment has completed an extensive renovation of the existing fabric, returning it to some of its former glory. The castle is open to the public every day.

Loch Awe is the south-east frontier of Lorn and is only a mile shorter than Loch Lomond, itself the largest area of fresh water in Britain. Loch Awe certainly ranks alongside Loch Lomond and Loch Maree as among the most beautiful of Scottish freshwater

FORT WILLIAM - TAYNUILT

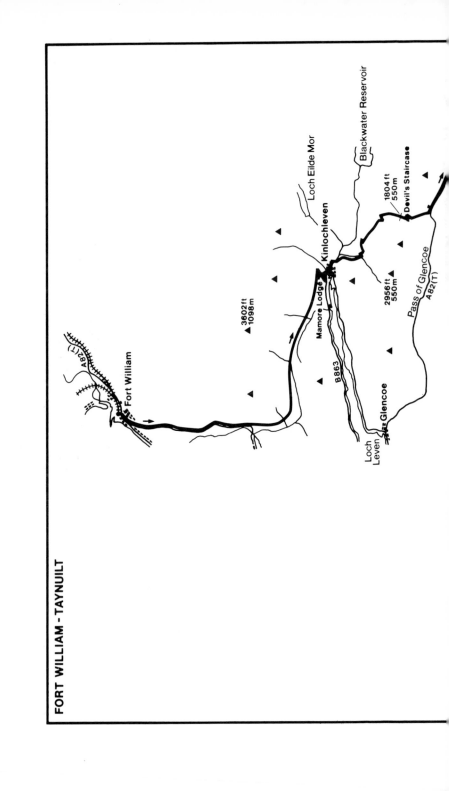

Blackwater Reservoir

Loch Eilde Mor

1804 ft
550 m

Devil's Staircase

Kinlochleven

2956 ft
550 m

Pass of Glencoe

A82(T)

Mamore Lodge

3602 ft
1098 m

B863

Glencoe

A82(T)

Fort William

Loch
Leven

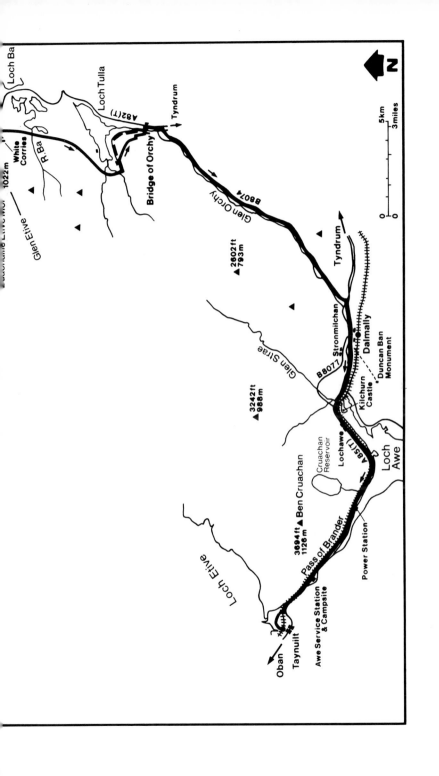

Glen Coe

lochs. Loch Awe village was famous during Victorian times as the chief point of embarkation for visitors to the many mansions built around the lochside by rich sporting gentry who spent the 'season' shooting and fishing in the surrounding countryside. The original old steamer pier is next to the railway station and from here you can take cruises around the loch.

The mountain to the right of the road along Loch Aweside is Beinn Cruachan − 3,689 feet (1,124m) high and eighteen miles (28.96km) in circumference. At mile 44.83 is the Cruachan Hydro Electric station − they have conducted tours in a mini-bus which takes visitors deep into the heart of the mountain. The Cruachan scheme was opened in 1965 and was the second biggest of its kind in the world (the biggest was in Luxembourg). Past the hydro scheme Loch Awe narrows into the pass of Brander, its Gaelic name, Am Bramraidh, means 'Place of Ambush', and a perfect site it is for such a strategy. It was the scene of Robert the Bruce's revenge on the MacDougalls, when he routed and killed many of them and gave a large part of their territory to Campbell of Loch Awe. Here too, passed that under-rated military genius, the Duke of Montrose, in his astonishing winter campaign of 1644/5 which commenced with the sacking of Inveraray Castle and ended at Inverlochy on Candlemass Day with an overwhelming victory over a combined force of Campbells and Lowlanders. From this battle's terrible toll, the Campbells as a fighting force were never to recover.

There is a barrage across the river here which has an electric lift to carry the salmon and sea trout thirty feet up to the top where they are released into the loch. This enables the fish to reach the higher reaches of the river system where they spawn. There is a lay-by just past the dam and from May to October this is a good vantage point to see the salmon jumping as they wait to go up in the lift.

Taynuilt, in Gaelic Tigh-an-Allt, means 'house by the burn'. The village is situated between the main road (A85 T) and the shores of Loch Etive. Worth a visit is the Bonawe Furnace which has been recently restored. It used to be an iron-smelting furnace set up in 1753 by Richard Ford of the Newland Company of Coniston, Lancashire. The iron ore was imported from Cumberland by three-masted sailing ships and water which had been ingeniously diverted from the River Awe drove the great iron water wheel which powered two large pairs of bellows to provide a continuous blast to the furnace. The works proved especially valuable during the Napoleonic Wars when cannon and munitions were in great demand. The furnace closed in 1879.

Map: OS Landranger nos. 41 and 50

Distance: 59.29 miles, 95.39 kilometres

Difficulty: the first half is challenging, the last half easy

Time: 2 days minimum, worth taking longer

Logistics: by train to Fort William or by car on the main road (A82 T).

Route Description
38.67 miles (62.22km) of tarmac; 20.62 miles (33.17km) of track.

This tour incorporates breathtaking scenery, a rich history and a challenging yet enjoyable variety of track. An especially good feature of it is that it is rideable during and after heavy rain, as there are bridges over the larger burns and rivers. But one must also take into account the fact that much of this route is very exposed, with few places to escape from the elements.

The tour begins at the railway station in Fort William and from there proceeds out of town on an up-and-down (mostly up) single track road, rising from sea level to 328 feet (100m). At this point, the road joins the West Highland Way and becomes track. From here to Kinlochleven is fairly easy riding; well-maintained track climbing gradually to a summit at 984 feet (300m), followed by a long and delicious downhill. Enjoy it because immediately after Kinlochleven you encounter an uphill guaranteed to make you question your sanity. The track rises from Kinlochleven (services and bunkhouse) at sea level to 1,804 feet (550m) in under four miles. For the last mile of this hill it deteriorates to rough trail and reaching the summit involves pushing, pulling, carrying and cursing your bike. The view from the summit is literally breath-taking − that is if you have any left by now! Glen Coe stretches away to the right, the start of Rannoch Moor to the left and the mighty Buchaille Etive Mór directly in front of you: this is big country.

A short, steep descent down the Devil's Staircase, followed by a restful four miles of tarmac, brings you to White Corries, a winter ski resort. The chair-lift operates all year round (weather permitting) and the view from the top makes this a worthwhile diversion. Also here is the Kingshouse Hotel − bicycle friendly and bar food. Biking through Blackmount, one is surrounded by the very finest Scotland has to offer; the track varies from good to excellent, with some especially fun cobbled downhills − hang on to your loose bits here!

Despite an over-abundance of Forestry Commission trees in Glen Orchy, they are not yet tall enough to hide the beauty of this glen and the ride down it is delightful. The road is single track and for the lower half of the glen stays close to the river, giving one endless places for stopping for a picnic. If you stop to admire the waterfalls at mile twenty-nine beware of the slippery rocks, especially if the river is in spate. The route then joins the A85(T) and returns to Taynuilt via Dalmally and Loch Awe.

Ben Cruachan at dawn

NOT to be missed on this tour − Shore Cottage Tearoom in Taynuilt, this offers the ultimate in home baking and Scottish hospitality, try everything, try and stop yourself trying everything! Also, at mile 56.47, follow the sign to the Inverawe Smokery and try their smoked rainbow trout. It comes in 4oz and 8oz ready-sliced vacuum packs, is cheaper than smoked salmon and much more delicious.

Route log

0.00m (00.00km) Fort William station. Exhibition of the West Highland Railway (seasonal), tearoom. Take the underpass to the town centre.

00.08 (00.12) Nevisport, mountaineering clothes, good coffee shop. Go straight on up the High Street.

00.58 (00.93) Roundabout, take the left turn, start ascent.

01.32 (02.12) Cattle grid, end of residential area.

01.58 (02.54) Summit.

03.38 (05.43) Telephone box.

05.25 (08.44) Fork, take left turn onto the West Highland Way. End of tarmac.

05.33 (08.57) Trail joins on the left, information map. Keep straight through the forestry.

06.40 (10.29) End of forestry, sheep fank, grubby little shelter full of sheep shit to stand and write notes in!

08.80 (14.16) Footbridge or ford.

11.49 (18.48) Fork. Turn right for West Highland Way trail − very steep white-knuckle downhill − or stay left for slightly longer way down which remains track. Mamore Lodge one mile − bar, cups of tea, B&B.

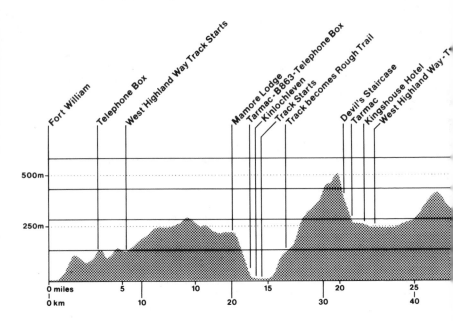

12.47 (20.06) Mamore Lodge — strange place but friendly, track becomes partial tarmac and very steep.

13.13 (21.12) West Highland Way trail joins track, turn left onto trail.

13.18 (21.20) Bear right.

13.46 (21.65) Tarmac, B863, turn left.

13.70 (22.04) Telephone box.

13.89 (22.34) Fork after the bridge, right turn for town centre and services and West Highland Lodge bunkhouse — hot showers, pool table etc. Left turn to return to the West Highland Way — the signpost says toilets. Go past them and follow the road around the back of the aluminium smelter.

14.23 (22.89) End of tarmac, turn right towards the pipes.

14.25 (22.92) The north-bound West Highland Way joins on the left, keep straight on over the bridge over the pipes.

14.30 (23.00) Bridge, bear left. Information map.

14.57 (23.44) Fork, keep right.

15.41 (24.79) Fork, go left.

15.50 (24.94) Bridge below dam.

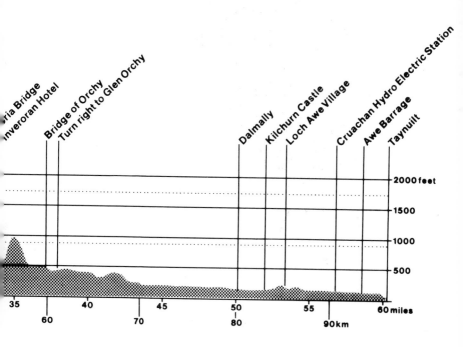

Loch Etive from Taynuilt

16.15 (25.98) Turn right onto rough trail.

17.95 (28.88) Summit, steep descent down the Devil's Staircase.

18.96 (30.70) Tarmac, turn left on A82(T).

19.08 (30.89) Choice of routes − stay on the A82(T) or turn left back onto the West Highland Way; for two miles it is quite boggy and there are stiles to cross. The log stays on tarmac.

20.76 (33.40) Turn left to Kingshouse Hotel − alternative route straight on.

21.53 (34.64) West Highland Way joins here.

21.56 (34.69) Kingshouse Hotel, take the south drive with the road closed notice.

22.54 (36.26) Turn left onto the A82(T) then almost immediately right to White Corries. Alternative route joins here.

22.97 (36.96) Turn left back onto the West Highland Way, opposite white cottage. End of tarmac.

23.05 (37.08) Take the right fork, start ascent.

24.47 (39.37) Summit.

25.74 (41.41) Bà Cottage ruin on the right, keep straight.

27.07 (43.55) Start of cobbled track − hang onto false teeth!

29.90 (48.10) Fork, keep straight.

30.65 (49.31) Gate, stile and crossroads.

31.22 (50.23) Victoria Bridge.

31.53 (50.73) Inveroran Hotel − bicycle friendly, bar, food.

31.59 (50.82) Fork, turn right for the steep ascent on the West Highland Way; alternative route for the less masochistic, keep straight and follow tarmac A8005 to Bridge of Orchy, three miles. This log turns right.

32.50 (52.29) Summit.

32.98 (53.06) Cross stile into forestry.

33.47 (53.85) Cross stile out of forestry.

33.84 (54.44) Gate. Tarmac. Straight over bridge to the main road (A82 T) and turn right — or, if you wish to end the tour here, the railway station is straight ahead, up the steep brae.

34.61 (55.68) Turn right down Glen Orchy.

37.50 (60.33) River Orchy waterfalls — dangerous rocks.

41.59 (66.91) Catnish picnic site.

44.70 (71.92) Junction with A85(T), turn right.

46.50 (74.81) Dalmally Hotel, not bicycle friendly, postbox. Alternative route on the right via Stronmilchan — 3.3 miles (5.31km), otherwise keep straight.

46.76 (75.23) Fork left for Dalmally village, pub, post office, railway station, good craft shop and excellent B&B at Cruachan House, otherwise keep straight.

48.11 (77.40) Left fork to Glasgow, keep straight.

48.33 (77.76) On the left, path to the ruined Kilchurn Castle — open to the public every day and well worth a visit.

48.85 (78.59) Alternative Stronmilchan route rejoins here.

49.79 (80.11) Loch Awe village, pub, post office, shop and loch cruises.

50.29 (80.91) St Conan's Kirk.

50.59 (81.39) Awe Filling Station — telephone, sweets and ice cream.

53.05 (85.35) Cruachan Hydro Electric Station — tours into the mountain.

55.34 (89.04) Awe Barrage — good place to watch the salmon jumping.

56.29 (90.57) Awe Service Station campsite etc..

56.47 (90.86) Right turn to Inverawe Smokery, keep straight.

56.51 (90.92) Bridge over River Awe.

58.30 (93.80) Fork. Turn right, signposted Brochroy.

58.89 (94.75) Fork. Turn right for Shore Cottage Tearoom, pier and boat trips. Bear left for Taynuilt main village, shops and railway station.

59.29 (95.39) Turn right in the village for the railway station (Oban-Glasgow line).

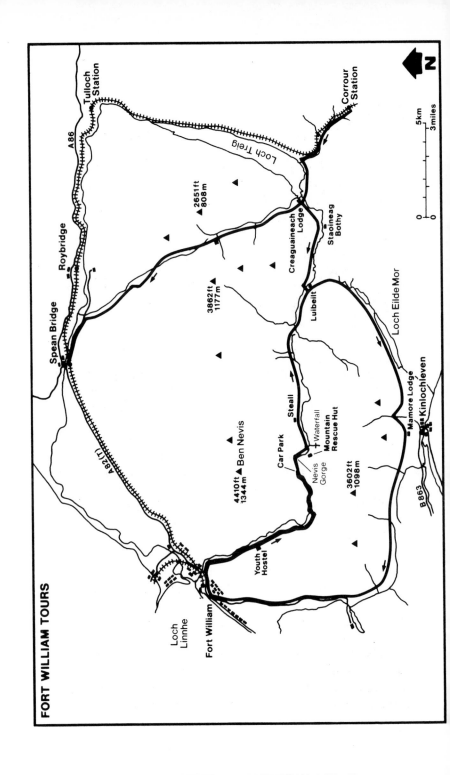

FORT WILLIAM TOURS

3

Corrour – Fort William

For Area information about Corrour, please see Routes 4 and 5.

Map: OS Landranger no. 41

Distance: 20.50 miles, 33.00 kilometres

Difficulty: challenging

Time: one day

Logistics: train to Corrour from Glasgow on the West Highland line. No access to Corrour by car.

Route description
13.70 miles (22.00km) track/trail. 6.80 miles (10.94km) tarmac.

This is a strenuous route that involves much pushing and carrying of the bike. It should not be attempted with any load or when the rivers are in spate. Even in the best conditions, this route is more pushing and carrying than riding.

Starting at Corrour station, cross the line and take the trail heading north with the railway line on your right. The trail soon becomes rough track and drops steeply down to the shores of Loch Treig. All too soon (mile 3.80) the route leaves Loch Treig and becomes trail to Luibeilt. Although the trail to Luibeilt and Glen Nevis is signposted before crossing the bridge (south side of the river), the trail up the north side – as indicated on the OS map – is much easier going. This does mean fording the river at Luibeilt but the savings in frustration are well worth it and you are going to get wet anyway. This portion of the route is quite boggy and rocky in places so be prepared to walk. Midway between Loch Treig and Luibeilt is a good bothy, a great spot to have a cup of tea and escape the elements.

At Luibeilt a decent track heads south to Kinlochleven (see Fort William Loop tour, p.13), and if you are tired of the difficult riding conditions you might consider turning left here. Remember, however, that this will increase your total miles and time so know your limits.

From Luibeilt the trail proceeds to the headwaters of the Water of Nevis and then down Glen Nevis to the Mountain Rescue club hut which can be reached (if desired) by crossing a fun three strand cable bridge. Fortunately it is not necessary to negotiate it with your bike.

The trail from the Mountain Rescue hut to the car park (mile 13.70) is very steep, rocky and unrideable. This is not the place to have an attack of vertigo: use extreme care while traversing this stretch of trail. From the car park it's a downhill, tarmac cruise through Glen Nevis, past the youth hostel and into Fort William.

This is a great ride but plan on being tired at the end of the day. If your idea of carrying your bike is getting it out of the train onto the platform, you might want to consider another route.

Route Log

00.00m (00.00km) Corrour station. There are two places to stay at this lonely outpost, Morgan's Den Bunkhouse (tel. 039785-236) and the Loch Ossian Youth Hostel which is one mile east of the station.

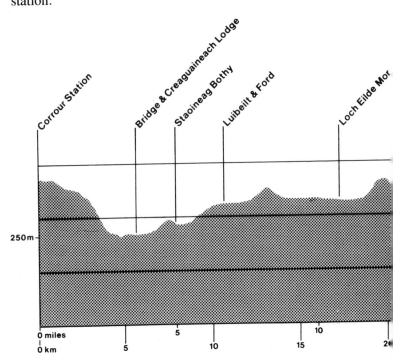

03.80 (06.11) Bridge and Creaguaineach Lodge. For the better trail cross bridge and turn left.

05.00 (08.00) Bothy, well worth a stop. Signed Staoineag on the OS map. The river can be forded here (unless in spate) if you wish to change banks.

06.95 (11.18) Luibeilt. Junction with track to Kinlochleven. A strange and unappealing ruin but dry. The river can be forded a short way upstream. Again this would be impossible when in full spate.

09.40 (15.12) Headwaters of Water of Nevis at Tom an Eite (1,319 feet, 402m).

12.30 (19.80) Ruin and bridge.

12.90 (20.75) Three cable bridge to the Mountain Rescue hut and base of waterfall. Don't worry, you do not need to cross it with your bike but it is well worth negotiating to see the waterfall. From hereon be prepared to carry the bike.

13.70 (22.00) Car park and tarmac.

18.00 (29.00) Glen Nevis Youth Hostel.

19.90 (32.00) Junction with A82(T), turn left to Fort William.

20.50 (33.00) Fort William station.

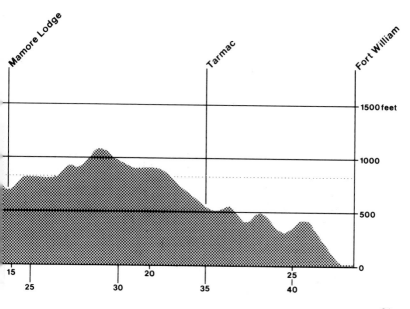

The track from Corrour to Spean Bridge

4

Corrour – Spean Bridge

Area information

Part of the pleasure of these tours is travelling to the starting point on the West Highland Railway line, surely one of the most beautiful train journeys in Britain.

The line was opened in 1894 to Fort William and later extended to Mallaig. The section between Bridge of Orchy and Corrour stations crosses Rannoch Moor and could only be built by 'floating' the line on a mattress of tree roots, larch saplings, sheep fleeces and thousands of tons of earth and ash. Because this section was so long they built a small station called Gorton where trains could pass each other. It was so remote and the surrounding moor so flat that the station master and his family had to have fresh water delivered by train in huge milk churns. The children went to school in an old carriage which was situated at the other end of the platform from the house. As the railway became modernised and timetables changed, this passing place was no longer needed and it has now been demolished.

Rannoch station, opened on August 3rd, 1894, was built to the design of Charles Forman. Right in the middle of the moor, Rannoch and Corrour are the two most romantic, isolated stations on the whole system. When the railway companies wanted to build their Highland line through part of Corrour Forest, the owner, Sir John Stirling-Maxwell, gave permission on two conditions: the first that a station be provided at which his guests might leave the train and the second that the station would never close for as long as his family remained at Corrour. Thus visitors to the lodge would alight from the train and be conveyed to Loch Ossian by pony and trap where they would embark on a steam yacht for the three mile voyage to the lodge. The station remained private until September 15th, 1934 when it was opened to the public. Corrour is the highest station on the line, at 1,476ft (450m).

Spean Bridge seems positively suburban compared to Rannoch and Corrour. Not only is it a station for the West Highland line, but it was from here on July 22nd, 1903 that the ill-fated line to

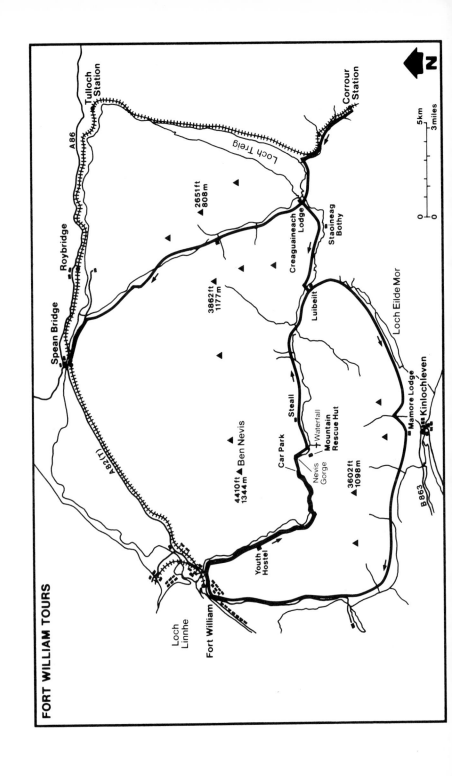

FORT WILLIAM TOURS

Fort Augustus was opened. The first closure came in 1906 when the extension to the Fort Augustus pier closed and then in 1911 all traffic on the line came to a halt because of lack of funds. The line re-opened in 1913 only to close again twenty years later. Probably the most disastrous railway line of all time, it often grossed little more than a thousand pounds a year.

The bridge in the name Spean Bridge was built by Thomas Telford in 1819. This remarkable engineer was born the son of a shepherd in Dumfriesshire in 1757 and was virtually self-taught. He designed the Götha Canal in Sweden, the Caledonian Canal (which runs from Fort William to the North Sea) and built numerous roads, bridges, docks and harbours throughout Scotland and Wales. He died in 1834 and is buried in Westminster Abbey.

Two miles west of Spean Bridge there are the remains of another bridge, the work of General Wade in 1736. It was built over a gorge a hundred feet above the river and was part of the military road that linked Fort William to Fort Augustus. Nine years later Bonnie Prince Charlie was to raise his standard at nearby Glenfinnan and a skirmish, probably one of the first of the '45 rising, took place by this old bridge.

During the Second World War the area surrounding Spean Bridge was used as a training ground for commandos, in commemoration of whom stands a superb monument on the hill just outside the village on the A82(T) main road.

Map: OS Landranger no. 41

Distance: 15.33 miles, 24.65 kilometres

Difficulty: challenging

Time: a short day if not camping

Logistics: By train to Corrour from Glasgow on the West Highland Line. No access to Corrour by car.

Route description
12.74 miles (20.49 km) track/trail, 2.59 miles (4.16km) tarmac.

British Rail run two kinds of passenger trains on this line; one is an engine with separate carriages and guards van, the other is the Super Sprinter which incorporates everything under one roof.

A good camping place (Corrour—Spean Bridge)

Your bicycle will travel free in the guards van of the larger train but on the Sprinter there is a charge (at the time of writing three pounds). In their information leaflet British Rail say that they reserve the right to refuse to carry a bicycle if there is no room on the train. On the larger trains this is not a problem but in the height of summer the Super Sprinter can be extremely crowded. I was never actually refused entry onto the train but if you are going to be travelling as more than one or two people it would be wise to organise train schedules accordingly. For British Rail information numbers see page 105.

From Corrour station cross the line and follow the trail heading north with the railway line on your right. It is slightly boggy in places but easy riding. At mile 1.39 the trail joins a rough track and shortly after descends to Loch Treig (check your helmet is firmly fixed). Treig in Gaelic means 'desolation' and with the lonely lodge at the western end it is a very apt description. The track turns to trail after crossing the bridge over Abhainn Rath and becomes ill-defined around the lodge. It picks up again as you head northwards to the sheep fank. This is classic glaciated terrain and after the fank the trail disappears into the most enchanting miniature gorge which wends its way to the top of the bealloch. The trail then keeps to the left of the burn Allt Na Lairige and from here until the bothy at mile 7.40 the only word I can think of to describe it is unprintable! The ascent is steep in some places and boggy in others; intermittent riding, pushing, carrying and plenty of swearing! But do not despair, this gives one plenty of time to see the wildlife which is abundant because of the remoteness of the area. As long as the wind is not at your back the deer should be plentiful; hinds will make a coughing noise to warn others of your approach and if you ride this at the beginning of October, the roarings of the stags at rutting time echoes among the rocks in the high corries. I saw a pair of Golden eagles, a sparrowhawk, grouse, snipe and blackcock and the trail is certainly high enough for ptarmigan. This most delightful of Scottish birds is rarely seen because it inhabits only the bleak, inhospitable tops of the mountains. It is the only British bird which changes colour with the seasons, passing through a complex series of moults from pure white in winter to mottled brown in summer with transitional stages in spring and autumn. In winter the bird's feathered feet act as snow shoes.

At mile 6.17, the terrain flattens out for a moment and there is a lovely pool in the burn — perfect for swimming — remember though that even in sunshine this water is at 1,312ft and may be colder than it looks. A good camping spot if you are taking your time. At mile 7.40 a bothy heralds the return to track and there is only one more small ascent before a downhill of which dreams are made. You descend from a height of 1,640 feet (500m) to 164 feet (50m) above sea level in almost seven miles, on excellent track with panoramic views northwards.

Return to earth at mile 12.74 with a gentle single track tarmac road into Spean Bridge — shops, tearoom, hotel, train station and main A82(T). If you are heading on to Fort William and do not like the thought of riding on the busy A82(T), then you can time your arrival here to catch the train into Fort William.

Note: I wanted to make this tour go to Fort William via the tram line you will see on your Landranger map, which would have been perfect. If you are thinking of doing this too, be warned: the OS

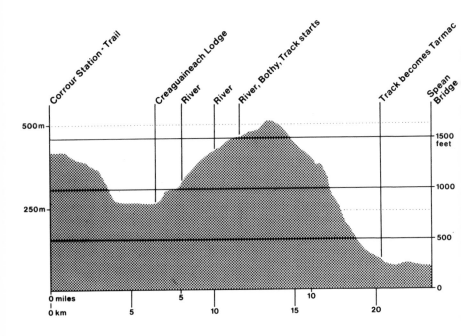

map has the bridges marked as being there but owing to someone unfortunately killing themselves while riding a motorbike along this stretch, they have been demolished and the track blocked, making it unsuitable for biking.

Route Log

00.00m (00.00km) Corrour Station. Cross track and head north on the trail.

01.39 (02.23) Trail joins track.

01.70 (02.73) Fork, keep straight.

03.89 (06.25) Trail to Glen Nevis on the left, keep straight across the bridge.

03.92 (06.30) Alternative trail to Glen Nevis on left, turn right.

03.96 (06.37) Lodge.

04.22 (06.78) Gate and sheep fank.

05.14 (08.27) Cross river.

06.17 (09.92) Good place to camp.

06.34 (10.20) Cross river.

07.40 (11.90) Cross river, bothy (locked), track begins.

08.53 (13.43) Summit.

10.50 (16.89) Forestry, gate.

11.45 (18.42) End of forestry, gate.

11.52 (18.53) Old tramway on the left (not rideable).

11.91 (19.16) Fork, keep straight.

12.52 (20.14) Gate.

12.74 (20.49) Turn left on tarmac.

14.18 (22.81) Keep straight.

15.33 (24.66) Junction, turn left for the station, right for Spean Bridge Hotel, pub, tearoom, woollen mill, shop and main A82(T) to Fort William.

Ardverikie Lodge, Loch Laggan (Corrour — Rannoch)

5

Corrour — Rannoch Station

Area information
This tour takes you past Loch Ossian, one of the highest lochs in Scotland at 1,268 feet (387m), through Corrour Estate and the Forestry Commission down to Loch Laggan which is a mere 820 feet (250m) above sea level. The beauty of this loch has been spoilt by the dam at the Spean Bridge end but the surrounding mountains more than make up for this.

The loch was once known as Lagganchoinnich, Loch of Kenneth's Hollow, from the tiny church of St Kenneth, the ruins of which can still be seen. At mile twenty-three you can see Ardverikie Lodge on the opposite side of the loch — an estate famous for its association with royalty. The name Ardverikie is said to mean 'the residence of Fergus' (an ancient king of Scotland). One of the islands in the loch is called Eilan-an-Righ, the King's Island. Queen Victoria stayed there in 1847 and considered buying it before she decided Balmoral was nicer. The famous artist Landseer often stayed there and the lodge before the present one burnt down on the day he was buried.

At the top of Glen Pattack is the magnificent Ben Alder, at 3,767 feet (1,148m) as high as the Monadhliath range. This remote and mysterious mountain is the centre of Ben Alder Forest — a famous deer forest, which was created as such in 1838.

To make a deer forest in those days was quite simple — provided one had the money. All one had to do was buy a large piece of hill ground, build a suitable house, clear the ground of sheep and wait for the numbers of deer to build up. In 1854 a rich industrialist bought nine thousand acres (3,643ha) of deer forest for twelve thousand pounds and in 1859 bought another twenty-two thousand acres (8,906ha) adjoining his estate for thirty-six shillings an acre. The heyday of Highland deer stalking was between 1880 and 1910. With the price of wool and mutton falling sharply, the rents of sheep farms were forced down and with sporting leases in ever-growing demand, the sheep were cleared off the ground and the amount of land reserved for deer went up and up. By 1890 there

CORROUR - RANNOCH STATION

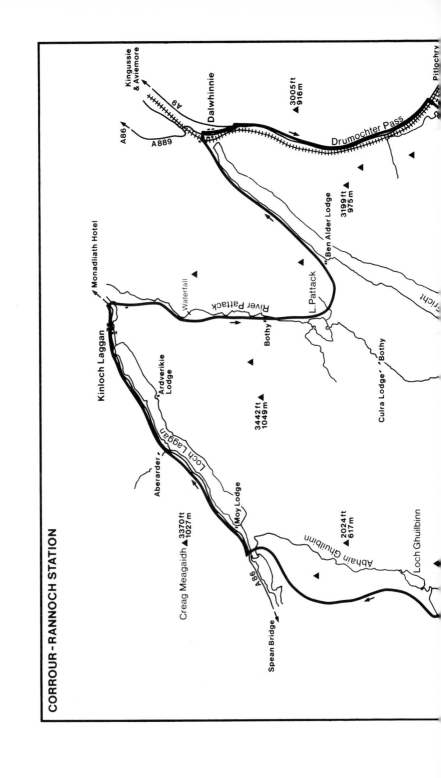

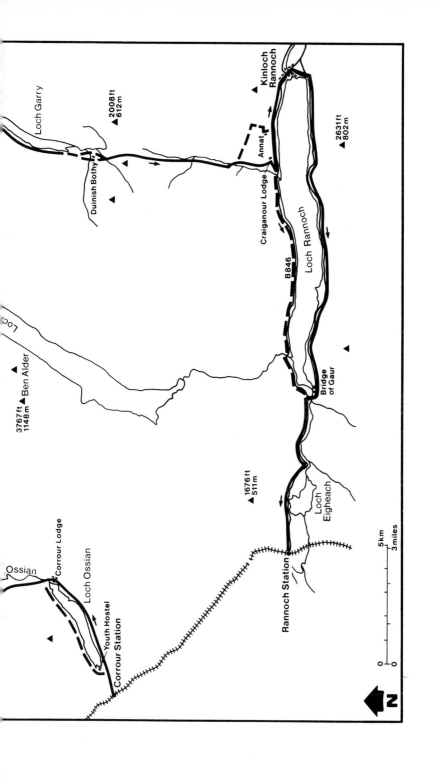

were one hundred and thirty deer forests in Scotland covering two and a half million acres (1m ha.).

Bonnie Prince Charlie hid on the lower slopes of Ben Alder in 'Cluny's Cage', overlooking Loch Ericht, before his escape to France. One of his followers, Cluny MacPherson, chief of the clan Chattan shot his last stag here before leaving the country to join the Prince in exile. Loch Ericht is one of the most solitary lochs in Scotland, fifteen miles (24km) long and in some places extremely deep.

Dalwhinnie, the first village on this tour, claims to be one of the highest in Scotland at 1,169 feet (356m) above sea level. It cannot have changed much since described in Murray's 1894 Handbook for Scotland as 'a desolate and solitary spot, protected by a few fir trees from the cold winds'. It must have been a cheerless stopover for the sheep and cattle drovers in those days, especially with the cold comfort of the Drumochter Pass (1,516 feet, 462m, log mile 45) to come. The name Dalwhinnie is a corruption of the Gaelic meaning 'dell of the meeting'. Highland chiefs often met here to talk or (as seems much more common in Highland history) to fight to the death. General Wade was busy here in 1732, building the road from Cullachy through the Corrieyairack Pass. Twenty-two miles were completed in six months, an amazing achievement when compared with road construction of today. The village has all services and also a fine distillery which does excellent tours. Apart from its own pure malt it is the home of Long John blended whisky.

Map: OS Landranger nos. 41 and 42

Distance: 75.85 miles, 122.38 kilometres

Difficulty: easy

Time: two to three days

Logistics: Train to Corrour station from Glasgow on the West Highland line. Vehicle access to Rannoch station by single track road on the B846. No car access to Corrour.

Route description

39.75 miles (63.95km) track; 36.10 miles (58.43km) tarmac.

We suggest biking the route as it is logged because the hills are more favourable than if you do it the other way round. Services

Peat-eating in Skye

are few and far between on this tour and we would not only suggest carrying some supplies with you but also making the detour (see log mile 24.30) to the Monoliadth Hotel — bicycle friendly, good plain food, sandwiches to take away — before heading up to Ben Alder.

In the whole of this tour there is only one bad piece of trail and that is at log mile 50.26 and lasts for three-quarters of a mile. Otherwise the tracks used on this route are superb. The scenery becomes increasingly spectacular, especially riding up by the River Pattack, culminating in breathtaking views of Ben Alder. There then follows a fun downhill all the way to Dalwhinnie and its distillery. This does an interesting tour lasting half an hour with the bonus of a free dram at the end. This should be kept until the A9 trunk road has been negotiated. Extreme caution is needed on this stretch and it is not suitable for children. Expect a surprise between Loch Garry and Loch Rannoch in the shape of Duinish bothy, a lovely place to stop. The tour concludes along the south side of Loch Rannoch with a gentle ascent to the station. While the stretch on the A9 is unfortunate, the rest of this tour more than makes up for it. The superior quality of the tracks and the diversity of landscape made this one of my favourites and one to recommend strongly.

If you are a bicycling family but feel your children are too young to cope with either the length of this tour or the A9, a lovely day tour is to bicycle from Corrour to the River Ossian (log mile 6.24) which is a wonderful picnic spot and return to the station via the track on the other side of Loch Ossian.

Route Log

00.00m (00.00km) Corrour station, no services. Morgan's Den Bunkhouse − tel. no. 039785-236. Take the only track heading east.

01.56 (02.51) Fork. Turn right. The left fork is an alternative route along the north shore of Loch Ossian. Youth Hostel visible on the lochside.

01.74 (02.79) Turning to Loch Ossian Youth Hostel. Open May 15th to October 1st. No vehicles, no shops, advance booking recommended.

04.00 (06.43) Fork, go left.

04.13 (06.64) Bridge and Corrour Lodge.

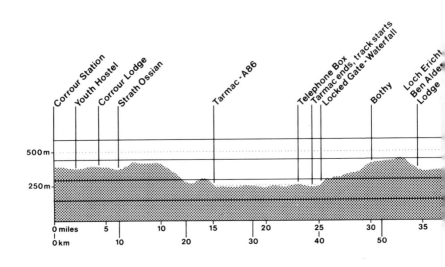

04.32 (06.95) Fork, go right — alternative north route meets here. Memorial stone.

06.24 (10.00) Fork, stay left. On the right, footbridge across River Ossian to ruin. Strath Ossian cottage and Loch Ghuilbuinn.

09.66 (15.54) Cattle grid, forestry starts, begin descent.

12.33 (19.83) Fork, go right.

14.59 (23.47) Gate and bridge.

14.80 (23.80) Fork, go left.

14.97 (24.00) Gate, bridge and intersection with tarmac — A86. Turn right.

19.25 (31.00) Craig Meagaidh National Nature Reserve — birch woods, alpine flowers, eagles, buzzards, ptarmigan, dotterel and snow bunting.

22.71 (36.54) Petrol station, limited food supplies.

23.27 (37.44) Ardverikie Estate Gatehouse and bridge on the right.

23.72 (38.16) Telephone.

24.30 (39.00) Right turn to Pattack and Loch Ericht. For food and services continue five miles on the A86, and on the junction of A86 and A889 is the Monoliadth Hotel — good, if plain food,

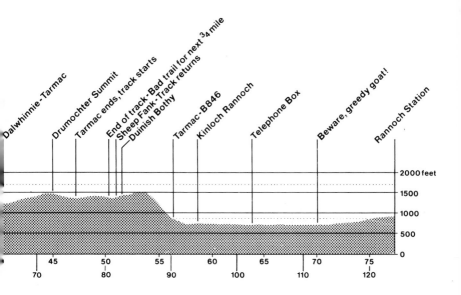

huge servings at very reasonable prices. They will make you sandwiches to take away if you want.

24.42 (39.29) Cross bridge and take right fork.

24.64 (39.64) Fork, go left and start ascent.

24.90 (40.00) Gallovie farmhouse.

25.56 (41.12) Locked gate, lift over or squeeze through. Magnificent waterfall 100yds down the path on the left, immediately after the gate.

26.89 (43.26) Fork, keep left following the river.

27.80 (44.73) Fork, keep left.

29.90 (48.10) To the left of the track is a footbridge over gorge and waterfall.

30.14 (48.49) Bothy, Blackburn of Pattack (see p.110).

30.49 (49.00) Locked gate in the middle of a bridge, lift over or swim. Track deteriorates until the next gate − 1.20 miles.

31.69 (51.00) Gate and Loch Pattack.

31.93 (51.37) Fork, stay left for Loch Ericht. Right track goes to Culra Lodge and bothy (see p.110).

32.16 (51.74) Pony shelter, start of descent to Loch Ericht.

32.89 (52.92) Gate (to spoil downhill run).

34.00 (54.70) Loch Ericht and Ben Alder Lodge, keep left.

37.67 (60.61) Gate, Dalwhinnie in view.

39.06 (62.84) Level crossing, tarmac road shortly after.

39.24 (63.13) Dalwhinnie train station.

39.35 (63.31) T-junction, hotels, shops, distillery. Turn right.

40.55 (65.24) T-junction − the A9, turn right. Use caution: busy main road for the next 6.39 miles.

45.30 (72.88) Drumochter summit, 1,516 feet (412m) above sea level. For quieter alternative route take the old road (gated) to Dalnaspidal − two miles.

46.94 (75.52) Turn right to Dalnaspidal.

46.97 (75.57) Turn left.

47.10 (75.78) Level crossing.

47.14 (75.84) Turn right over locked gate, track starts here.

47.44 (76.33) Bridge and dam.

49.54 (79.70) Hydro Electric station.

50.26 (80.86) Track ends, waterfall, good stopping place. Bad trail for the next ¾ mile.

51.04 (82.12) Ford the river by the sheep fank − if the river is in spate, there is a bridge ¼ mile upstream.

51.10 (82.21) Sheep fank and return of track.

51.32 (82.57) Duinish bothy.

51.39 (82.68) Standing stone, track from the bridge joins main track.

54.86 (88.26) Fork right to Loch Rannoch, alternative route to the left, 2.13 miles (3.43km), gated and boggy.

55.87 (89.89) Beautiful weeping-birch wood.

56.59 (91.05) Fork, turn right to main road.

56.92 (91.58) B846, for shorter route to the station turn right (8.2 miles: 13.1km). Otherwise turn left.

57.69 (92.82) Alternative hill route meets B846 at Annat House.

58.26 (93.74) Rannoch School of Adventure (in case you are not enjoying this one). Windsurfing, mountain bike hire — no repairs but emergency help possible.

58.87 (94.72) Kinloch Rannoch, all services.

59.02 (94.96) Turn right over the bridge for south Rannoch road and caravan/campsite with hot shower.

59.61 (95.91) Culmore cottage on the left, recommended restaurant and B&B.

61.70 (99.27) Kilvrecht campsite (Forestry Commission).

62.67 (100.83) Rannoch Forest walking area.

63.73 (102.54) Telephone box.

70.12 (112.82) Bridge of Gaur. Post office, telephone, shop. The shop is closed on Saturday and Sunday.

70.22 (112.98) Victoria Bridge — beware greedy goat!

70.46 (113.37) T-junction. Alternative route meets here, turn left.

72.91 (117.31) Power station.

74.34 (119.61) Public footpath to Fort William on the right — The Road to the Isles.

75.85 ((122.38) Rannoch station. Tearoom and post office on the station.

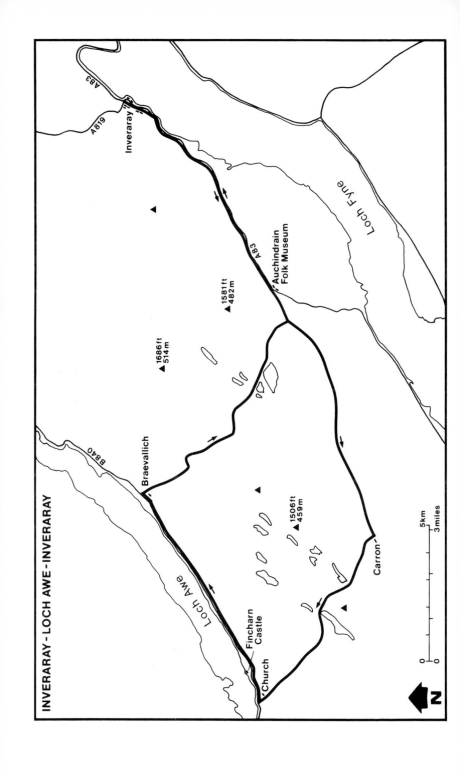

INVERARAY - LOCH AWE - INVERARAY

Inveraray

A83

A819

Loch Fyne

Auchindrain
Folk Museum

A83

▲1581ft
482m

▲1686ft
514m

BB40

Braevallich

Loch Awe

▲1506ft
459m

Fincharn
Castle

Church

Carron

N

5km
3miles
0
0

6

Inveraray – Loch Awe

Area information

This section of mid-Argyll has much to offer whether your interest lies in history, wildlife, botany, or just plain sightseeing. The main attraction of Inverarary is its castle. The present one was built in stages beginning in 1744 and took over forty years to be completed. It is the home of the Duke of Argyll, the present laird being the twelfth duke and twenty-sixth chief of the Clan Campbell. A 'fairy tale' castle, it is known for its armoury, china collection and tapestries, along with its eighteenth-century French furniture. It is open daily from April to October and is located at the north end of the town on the A83(T). Also in Inveraray is the jail, providing an informative and enjoyable display of a nineteenth-century prison, courtroom and exercise yard. Definitely worth a visit, it is open daily. The 126ft bell tower is of interest for it contains the second heaviest 'ring' of ten bells in the world, each inscribed with the name of a saint. The parish church in Inveraray is unique in that it has a dividing wall so that services could be performed in English and Gaelic simultaneously. Sadly there are very few Gaelic speakers left in this part of Scotland, so these services are no longer available. The church is open daily.

Argyll wildlife park is located two miles southwest of Inveraray on the A83(T). The emphasis here is on Scottish wildlife and it also houses one of Europe's largest collections of waterfowl. It is open daily. The Auchindrain Folk Museum, five and a half miles southwest of Inveraray, demonstrates many aspects of the crofting way of life. There is a craft shop here as well. It is open daily from Easter to September.

The track followed on this tour is one of the oldest and most famous hill tracks. At one time it linked the crofting township of Auchindrain on Loch Fyne with the once important, but now sadly ruined, church of St Columba on Loch Aweside. The church has an interesting claim to fame; there is supposedly a handprint of the devil, an odd group of circular indentations, on the inside of the left portal of the west doorway. They are said to have been made by the devil while attempting to seize a local tailor who had accepted a challenge to spend a night in the church.

The ruins of Finchairn castle stand on the shore of Loch Awe, half a mile northeast on the B840 from the church of St Columba. Park at the gate and walk across the field to reach the ruin. The ruin is believed to be of thirteenth century origin; history relates how, on the marriage of two of his young retainers, Lord Finchairn insisted on exercising the infamous *droit de seigneur,* an ancient custom giving the chief the right to spend the wedding night alone with the bride. The young groom was so enraged that he set fire to the castle, destroying it. It has remained a ruin ever since. Shortly before the summit, the hill route passes below a rocky bluff − Black Duncan's seat − where he used to lay in wait to ambush and rob unwary travellers.

Mid-Argyll is beautiful at any time of the year but if possible try to visit during the spring when the road and trail sides are ablaze with wild flowers. The primrose is in full bloom in May and as its delicate pale yellow colour fades the contrasting blue and sweet aroma of the bluebell (wild hyacinth) takes over. If you are fortunate you may see an early purple orchid; it stands up to a foot tall with a spike of bright purple flowers. Both the primrose and the orchid are protected species so please do not pick them. Be sure also to turn an occasional eye skywards as the magnificent osprey is known to frequent this area.

Map: OS Landranger nos. 55 and 56

Distance: 35.11 miles, 56.50 kilometres

Difficulty: challenging, with some very rough stretches

Time: one full day

Logistics: The nearest train station is at Dalmally, approximately 15 miles from Inveraray (via the A85(T) and A819). The direct route from Dalmally to Inveraray is a very pretty ride (tarmac), and another fine, though mostly tarmac loop, is from Dalmally to Inveraray (A85(T), A819) then over to Loch Awe via this tour and back to Dalmally along the shore of Loch Awe (B840 single track tarmac). There is a regular bus service to Inveraray but at the time of writing, not many companies will carry bicycles. Always check first. We suggest you ride this tour in the direction indicated due to the nature of the climbs and descents.

Forestry track — the better sort

Route description
18.82 miles (30.28km) tarmac, 16.29 miles (26.22km) track/trail.

This is a mountain biker's mountain bike tour and is not for the faint-hearted. Once off the tarmac there is hardly a level foot; it is all up or down. There are some very technical descents which border on being almost unrideable − these are of course the most thrilling kind; at other points the descents are long, smooth and fast. The climbs are equally demanding; some due to gradient and trail conditions, others (one in particular) challenging your stamina by length alone. Besides excellent riding, this route also takes one through some wild and remote country. The section from the Carron ruin over to Loch Awe is particularly scenic as it passes several lochs and has yet to be covered with forestry. There are several picnic and rest areas along Loch Awe. However there are no shops once you leave Inveraray, so plan accordingly. This is a challenging and exhilarating tour − just don't forget your helmet!

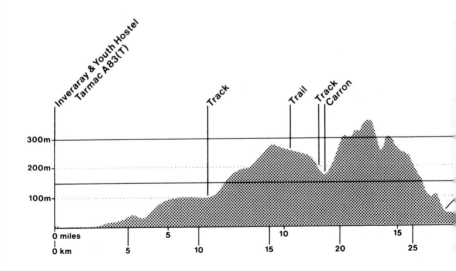

Route Log

00.00m (00.00km) Inveraray Youth Hostel.

00.25 (00.40) Inveraray — a tourist-orientated town, known primarily for its castle (seat of the Duke of Argyll), bell tower, and jail (excellent tour). There are several tearooms, pubs, hotels along with a bank and a post office. The Youth Hostel is a good source of information for cyclists. From Inveraray head south on the A83(T).

01.75 (02.81) Argyll Wildlife Park. Many Scottish as well as other wildlife on display in a zoo-like setting. Nominal fee, tea room.

02.75 (04.42) Argyll caravan park and campground. Bikers welcome. Small shop and hot showers.

05.86 (09.42) Turn right on tarmac, signposted Auchindrain; also signposted public footpath to Durran. At this junction is the Auchindrain Folk Life Museum, depicting life in a Scottish village in the mid 1800s. An interesting and informative display, well worth the admission price. Closed on Sundays.

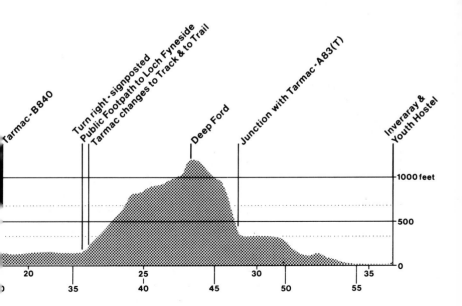

06.56 (10.55) Junction with footpath to Durran. If you have a car and do not wish to ride the tarmac from Inveraray, an excellent all dirt (and peat and water and rock) loop can be started here.

06.86 (11.00) End of tarmac, begin track through forestry.

10.46 (16.83) Track ends, begin trail.

11.60 (18.66) Beautiful old stone arch bridge, a real surprise and treat to come across. Sheep fank on the right. Trail becomes rough track at this point.

11.90 (19.14) Carron (ruin). Short strenuous climb.

12.10 (19.46) Gate.

13.56 (21.81) Summit and two small lochs. A spectacular view can be had by walking south-west along the ridge to Sidh Mor (see OS map). It is worth the walk. Begin EXTREME, white-knuckle descent at this point!

14.06 (22.62) End of descent, ford burn. Loch Gaineanhach on the left.

14.20 (22.84) Ford burn — a wet crossing probable.

14.50 (23.33) Begin climb.

14.75 (23.73) Summit.

14.90 (23.97) Short, steep descent.

15.55 (25.00) View of Loch Awe. Begin long descent.

16.15. (26.00) Gate.

16.48 (26.50) Four-way junction; continue straight on faint track.

16.62 (26.74) Ford.

17.00 (27.35) Locked gate, stile to one side.

17.06 (27.45) Church ruins.

17.15 (27.60) Junction with tarmac B840; turn right.

17.75 (28.55) Gate on left leads to the ruins of Finchairn Castle on Loch Aweside. Signposted Finchairn on the right side of the road.

21.86 (35.17) Fishfarm on the left.

22.20 (35.72) Braevallich Nursery on the left. A large selection of rhododendrons and azaleas are grown here.

22.25 (35.80) Turn right on tarmac, signposted public footpath to Loch Fyneside. This is the start of a long (3.4 miles: 5.47km) mostly gradual uphill.

22.30 (35.88) Veer right on track.

22.35 (35.96) Gate; not usually locked. Follow trail heading left.

22.42 (36.00) Stile over fence, then follow obvious trail right.

22.60 (36.36) Footpath joins track. Turn right and continue uphill

25.70 (41.35) Turn right on trail, signposted Auchindrain. This sign is fairly small and easy to miss. Keep a sharp eye out.
Note: for an excellent view of the area, continue less than one mile up the track to the summit, leave your bike here and climb the small peak to the left (An Suidhe, 1,686ft, 514m).

25.88 (41.64) Footbridge over small burn. The next mile of trail is the poorest of this tour, being quite boggy in places.

27.25 (43.84) Begin rough track at Loch Leacann.

27.65 (44.50) Ford Leacann water. This can be a substantial (waist deep) crossing at times. It is deeper than it looks.

27.70 (44.57) Begin steep rocky descent.

28.55 (45.94) Junction with tarmac. You can loosen your grip now . . . At this point you are where you were at mile 6.56 of this log. To complete this loop retrace your path to Inveraray and the Youth Hostel.

35.11 (56.50) Inveraray Youth Hostel.

7

Camasunary – South Skye

Area information

The Gaels called Skye 'the Winged Isle' (Eilean a Sgiathanach), a reference to its shape. If you glance at the map, you will see that the northern promontories, Waternish and Trotternish, look like two wings. But the Vikings, approaching by sea, saw a land heavily covered with cloud and named it Sküyo (pronounced Skya), the 'Cloud Island'.

According to historians, the Vikings completely devastated Skye around 800AD. Later, however, they arrived not as invaders but as refugees from troubles in their own homeland and for four hundred years Skye lay under their rule.

Skye is principally an agricultural island although tourism is fast catching up as the major cash-earner. The predominant form of farming is called crofting, a croft being a smallholding of between one and fifty acres (20ha.), the tenure of which is strictly controlled by various Acts of Parliament. It was not always thus: the placid and homely appearance of these small farms conceals a harrowing past.

In the dying years of the eighteenth and the beginning of the nineteenth centuries, it was discovered by sheep farmers from the Borders that, contrary to everyone's belief hitherto, a certain breed of sheep called the North Country Cheviot was not only capable of surviving in the harsh Highland climate but would actually prosper. It sounded an innocuous discovery, even a beneficial one when the sheepmen, or 'Improvers' as they liked to be called, pointed out the increase in general wealth that would thereby be derived. Landowners alerted themselves; and the realisation soon dawned that ranching large numbers of sheep on their hills was indeed a most profitable occupation, far more so than the paltry rents that they received from their numerous crofters who traditionally used the grazings to maintain small black cattle for household consumption.

Commercial logic demanded that the cattle must go. And since

The Cuillins in Skye

the crofters knew nothing about sheep, had probably never seen one before, they and their families had to go too. Some landlords addressed themselves to the question of where all these unfortunate people might go, many did not. Animals were slaughtered, villages levelled to the ground and whole households thrown into the streets while their possessions were burned. This brutal passage of history is known as the Highland Clearances and even today is an emotive subject. The name of Patrick Sellar, factor to the Duke of Sutherland and an ardent Improver, is both remembered and reviled.

Coinciding with and largely arising from the Clearances, came famine and disease. For many of those now homeless and starving, the New World beckoned. Emigration became the only hope and men, women and children in their thousands left the lands of their fathers to seek new lives in America, Canada, Australia and New Zealand.

The counties of Sutherland and Caithness were the worst affected but in Skye alone, 1,740 writs of removal were served between 1840 and 1880. No less than 40,000 souls were involved and of those 7,000 chose to emigrate. Today, the island has only one quarter of its 1841 population of 23,000.

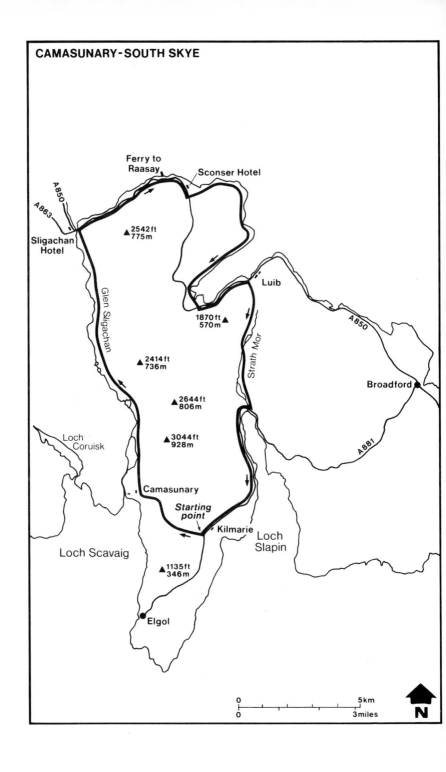

CAMASUNARY-SOUTH SKYE

Ferry to Raasay
Sconser Hotel
A850
A863
Sligachan Hotel
▲ 2542 ft 775 m
Glen Sligachan
Luib
A850
1870 ft ▲ 570 m
Strath Mor
Broadford
▲ 2414 ft 736 m
▲ 2644 ft 806 m
Loch Coruisk
▲ 3044 ft 928 m
A881
Camasunary
Starting point
Kilmarie
Loch Slapin
Loch Scavaig
▲ 1135 ft 346 m
● Elgol

0   5 km
0   3 miles

N

Nevertheless, crofting has survived and thanks to changes in the law, has even prospered in a modest sort of way in places like Skye. Another survival in the island is the Gaelic language which is still spoken by many and is in fact now being taught again in the schools.

Arriving at Kyle of Lochalsh, the Gateway to Skye, you cross to the island on the ferry. This is only a fifteen minute crossing although in the busy summer months you may have to queue for up to an hour before boarding. The ferry lands at Kyleakin where the castle Maol stands sentinel over the strait. Kyleakin gets its name from Hakon the Norse king whose fleet anchored here on the way to Largs in 1263. Taking the A850 you reach Broadford, an area full of interest to geologists on account of its abundance of fossils from the Cambrian and Jurassic Ages. At Broadford turn left onto the A881 which goes to Elgol. This is MacKinnon country and has been a prominent centre of religion since pre-historic times. There are at least five ruined churches or chapels, their graveyards containing prehistoric stones which probably belong to the pagan era. About a mile along this road there is the ruin of the old house, Coirechatachain, where Boswell and Dr Johnson were entertained by MacKinnon of Corry during their visit in 1773. At Torran there is a quarry where Skye marble is dug. This is believed to have been used in the Vatican and the Palace of Versailles as well as in the altar of Iona Abbey and various Scottish castles.

As the road winds its way round Loch Slapin, it passes Strathaird, now owned by the musician Ian Anderson (Jethro Tull). This was the hiding place of Bonnie Prince Charlie after he had travelled through Skye to Portree and then to the island of Raasay. This proved even more dangerous than Skye so Malcolm MacLeod escorted him back through the Cuillins and found him refuge with the chief of the clan MacKinnon. John MacKinnon hid the Prince in a cave on the shore of Loch Scavaig and after arranging a crossing to Mallaig landed the fugitive safely on the mainland on the night of the fourth of July 1746. MacKinnon was later betrayed and served a year's imprisonment for his part in the escape.

There is a fine view from here of the islands of Rhum and Eigg while in the far distance lies Soay, an island famous for sharks. The road ends at Elgol, where the views to the Black Cuillin and Soay are quite dramatic — as indeed are the views at mile 1.42 of the log which is not only a good stopping place to catch your breath after the steep ascent, but also a spectacular viewpoint overlooking Camasunary bay with the savage beauty of the Cuillin behind.

After bicycling through Glen Sligachan, one of the most impressive glens in Scotland, you reach the Sligachan Hotel which has been in the hands of the Campbell family for a century or more. Nestling below Glamaig it has always been a Mecca for climbers and artists and is certainly a welcome sight after the arduous miles just bicycled. We then turn right on the A850 passing the pier for the ferry to Raasay (a magical island which is well worth visiting, whether by bicycle or car). The route turns off the A850 at Luib whch has a small thatched museum. If you are planning a longer stay, or travelling by car, other places of interest to visit are; Dunvegan Castle, erected in the 9th century and the oldest inhabited castle in Scotland as well as the ancestral home of the Chiefs of the Macleod clan; the Clan Donald centre at Armadale which has won many awards for the splendour of its design and architecture; Portree, the capital village of Skye, and the old crofting village at Kilmuir known as the 'Skye Museum of Island Life', where a group of old thatched cottages make up an interesting museum of the past of a crofting community. I can recommend the food at the following places; the Pipers Moon tea-room at Luib (good scones); the Three Chimneys Restaurant at Colbost, by Dunvegan − delicious lunches and dinners (definitely need to book), and the Sconser Hotel for bar meals. There are many restaurants on Skye that cater for vegetarians − see p.108.

Map: OS Landranger no. 32
Distance: 29.62 miles, 47.65 kilometres
Difficulty: challenging
Time: a long one day, worth taking longer
Logistics: There are two main ferries to Skye: the first from Mallaig to Armadale, is summer only, not on Sundays at the time of writing, and it is recommended to book; the other, from Kyle of Lochalsh to Kyleakin, is further north but is only a fifteen minute sailing and is more frequent. So saying, at the height of the tourist season (end of July, August) the queue for this ferry may be an hour or more long. No booking is needed. Trains run to Kyle of Lochalsh via Inverness. From Armadale take the A851 sixteen and a half miles which then connects with the A850 to Broadford. From Kyleakin take the A850 to Broadford (nine and a half miles).

Turn left in Broadford (last services) and take the A881, signposted to Elgol, for 11.40 miles. If travelling by car there is space to leave it at the starting point, halfway up the hill by the locked gate. There are limited services three miles further along in Elgol — tearoom and shop.

Route description
15.70 miles (25.26 km) tarmac, 13.92 miles (22.39km) track/trail.

The route begins with a steep, rock-strewn ascent, followed by a precipitous, white-knuckle downhill to Camasunary Lodge. The view at the summit is breath-taking, overlooking Camasunary bay and Loch Na Crèitheach, with the Isles of Rhum and Soay to the south and the jagged peaks of the Black Cuillin mountains to the west. Past Camasunary Lodge is a bothy which can provide welcome shelter. Turn right just before the lodge. The track now becomes trail and although it deteriorates as it winds through Glen Sligachan the scenery most definitely does not. In fact this stretch of trail does everything to try and stop you looking anywhere else but down. A night camping by Lochan Dubha gives one time to explore Harta Corrie — a truly wild and remote place. The track continues in this manner all the way to Sligachan Hotel and the smoothness of tarmac beneath your wheels.

The route now follows tarmac until Luib — good coffee shop before another stretch of trail. Between Sligachan and Luib is the pier for the ferry to Raasay — definitely worth a day of exploration; outdoor adventure centre, ruined castle, abandoned mines, forest walks and fascinating geology. Be sure to ask the ferryman at what time the last ferry returns to Skye! Quarter of a mile south of the pier is the Sconser Hotel, bicycle friendly, good hot bar food and cold pints (not to mention hot baths, comfy beds and colour telly) and an exquisite wood-panelled dining room. Back to reality at Luib where the trail to the A881 is reminiscent of the Sligachan trail, only worse. Once back on the tarmac of the A881 the tour finishes with a long, gradual uphill and a fun downhill back to the starting point. This tour is for the adventurous and hardy who would consider pushing, lifting, sinking and swimming with bicycles fun. A rugged tour at any time, it is a real challenge when wet and should NOT be attempted when rivers are in full spate. If you are planning to do it in one day, start early.

Route Log

00.00m (00.00km) A881. Track starts. Map ref NG54.17, eleven miles from the Broadford turn-off. Locked gate, follow the track westwards.

00.67 (1.07) Start ascent − rugged.

01.42 (2.28) Summit, begin steep descent − check brakes.

02.51 (4.03) Camasunary Lodge, bothy, good beach. Turn right to Glen Sligachan by the ruined barn at the Lodge.

03.23 (5.19) Loch Na Crèitheach.

05.50 (8.84) Loch an Athain, good place to camp.

06.14 (9.87) Ford large burn (Allt nam Fraoch-Choire).

06.29 (10.12) Fork, Coruisk trail joins here.

06.45 (10.37) Lochan Dubha. Harta Corrie on the left.

08.40 (13.51) Ford large burn (Allt na Meassarroch).

09.72 (15.63) Sligachan Hotel in view.

10.12 (16.28) Tarmac, left 100 yds to Hotel − bar, food, telephone. Turn right on the A850.

13.32 (21.43) Pier, ferry point to Raasay.

13.87 (22.31) Sconser Hotel, an excellent place to stay, very helpful and friendly, good bar food, convenient for the ferry to Raasay.

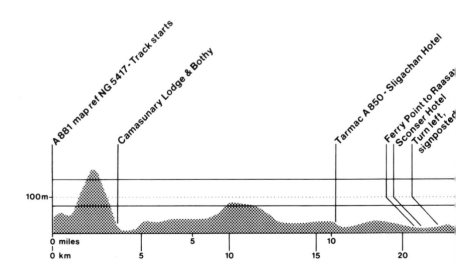

14.01 (22.52) Turn left, signposted to Moil. Golf course. For alternative shorter route continue on the A850 for 4.3 miles (6.92km).

14.05 (22.60) Quarry − caution, heavy machinery crossing the road.

19.62 (31.56) T-junction, rejoin A850, alternative route joins here. Turn left.

21.15 (34.00) Turn right to Luib. Telephone box and post box.

21.25 (34.19) Pipers Moon tearoom (good scones) sweets, post-cards, film, folk museum − 50p charge.

21.32 (34.40) Turn left. Take the path past the ruined cottage − the track is a potential alternative route, untested.

22.61 (36.37) Lochain Stratha Mhóir.

23.12 (37.20) Ford burn at the foot of the loch.

25.12 (40.41) T-junction, A881, turn right.

27.12 (43.63) Begin ascent.

28.12 (45.24) Summit, fun downhill to starting point − a good finish.

29.62 (47.65) Back at the starting point.

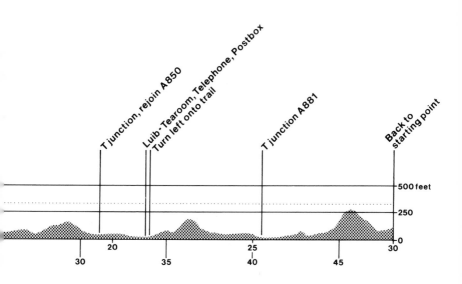

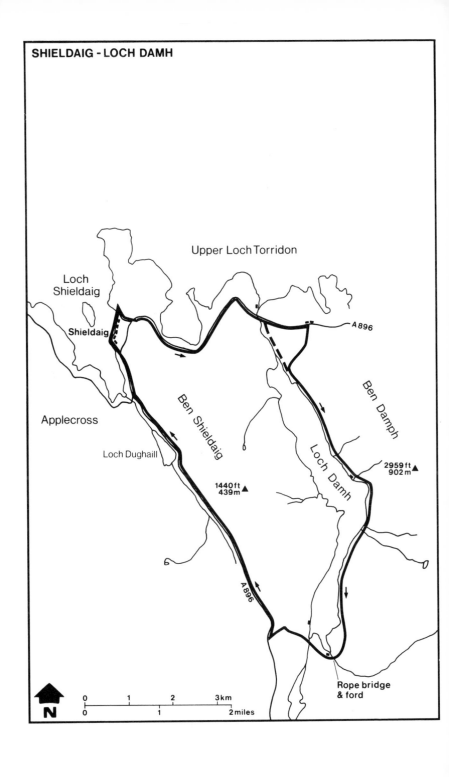

SHIELDAIG - LOCH DAMH

Upper Loch Torridon

Loch Shieldaig

Shieldaig

A 896

Applecross

Ben Shieldaig

Ben Damph

Loch Dughaill

Loch Damh

2959 ft
902 m ▲

1440 ft
439 m ▲

A 896

Rope bridge
& ford

N

| 0 | | 1 | | 2 | | 3 km |
| 0 | | | 1 | | | 2 miles |

8

Shieldaig – Loch Damh

Area information
Shieldaig is a picturesque little fishing village of whitewashed, mostly two-storeyed houses, which spread in a line along a shore of red sandstone. It lies between Ben Shieldaig, which rises to 1692ft (515m) and Loch Shieldaig which was once famous for its herring fishing. In the days of Norse rule it was given the name Sild-vik ('Herring Bay') from which the Gaelic Shieldaig is derived. The whole district was at one time renowned for illegal distilling of whisky. Offshore is Shieldaig island, twenty acres of Scots Pine that were planted in the middle of the nineteenth century. It was bought in 1970 by the National Trust and in 1974 it was adopted by two Americans who provide for its maintenance.

Map: OS Landranger no. 24

Distance: 14 miles, 22.55 kilometres

Difficulty: easy

Time: half day – day

Logistics: A896 to Shieldaig. No trains.

Route description
6.22 miles (9.65km) of track; 7.78 miles (12.90 km) of tarmac.

This is a gentle ride along the shore of Loch Damh with an excellent trail for most of the offroad section. An exciting rope bridge (too exciting for carrying bikes across) will ensure that at least one of you will get your feet wet; if the burn's in spate, it'll give you hairs on your chest as well. The tarmac section is a single track road, giving you a fun descent through Glen Shieldaig. The route takes you through some enchanting birch, oak and Caledonian pine woods with picnic and camping spots in abundance. The tour begins and ends in the picturesque village of Shieldaig – hotel, shop, post office. I was told it is possible to row out to explore Shieldaig island; the best place to enquire about this is the hotel or post office. If you are exploring the Applecross area then this is a lovely day's ride — suitable for all the family.

Route Log

00.00m (00.00km) Shieldaig Hotel — all services. Head north on tarmac through the village and up the hill.

00.15 (00.24) Junction with A896 — turn left.

02.59 (04.17) Cross bridge.

02.62 (04.22) Start of alternative route — 00.80 miles long. Keep straight.

03.31 (05.33) Turn right opposite house, end of tarmac.

03.39 (05.46) Gate.

03.81 (06.14) Alternative route joins track.

04.63 (07.46) Fish farm.

06.01 (09.68) The track ends at a house, trail starts.

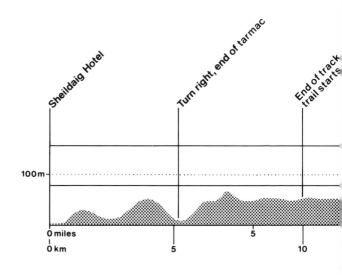

07.19 (11.58) Beach − good picnic area.

08.59 (13.83) Wood trail going left to Strath a' Bhathaich, keep straight on to the rope bridge and ford.

08.69 (14.00) Ford river at rope bridge. There is a possible four mile alternative route here starting on the left but the trail is ill-defined and boggy.

08.73 (14.05) Start ascent − half track, half tarmac.

08.83 (14.22) Fork, keep straight, right hand trail leads to fish farm.

09.53 (15.35) Junction with A896, turn right. (Alternative route rejoins here.)

09.86 (15.88) Summit. Fun descent through Glen Shieldaig.

13.45 (21.66) Junction with road to Applecross, good camping and picnic sites by the river.

14.00 (22.55) Take left fork back to Shieldaig.

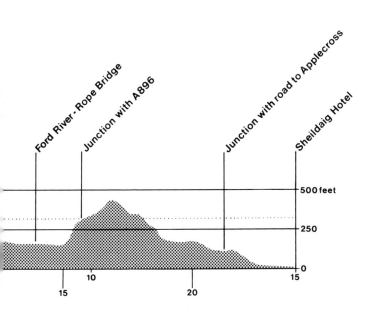

9

Glen Affric

Area information

Glen Affric lies to the west of Loch Ness and south of Glen Cannich and Glen Strathfarrar. These three glens are often linked together as being among the most beautiful in Scotland. with Glen Affric taking first prize. Affric certainly deserves such a high accolade, but with this and its easy access comes a high tourist penalty.

Two miles from Cannich the main road enters the Chisholms Pass and at Fasnakyle is the Hydro Electric station. When the Hydro flooded Loch Beinn a' Mheadhoin, the water level rose twenty feet submerging the old road. The new road leaves Strath Glass and climbs to the right of the loch revealing more and more of the grandeur of the glen. The birch woodland which fills it above and below Dog Falls is spectacular and the view westwards up Loch Affric must be one of the finest in Scotland.

These ancient forests supported various species of animal in the past. Bears are thought to have become extinct by the tenth century; the beaver lasted longer – it was known in Gaelic as Dobhran Losleathan, 'the broad-tailed otter'. Reindeer fared even better and survived until the twelfth or thirteenth century. The most tenacious survivor was the wolf and although it was vigorously persecuted throughout historic times, these old forests gave it an impenetrable retreat and not until they had been greatly reduced was the last wolf killed in the middle of the eighteenth century. From the earliest times wolves had prices on their heads – in 1491 the bounty on a skin was five shillings but by 1621 it had risen to six pounds, thirteen shillings and four pence.

In the eighteenth century Glen Affric was a flourishing timber producing area, the logs being floated down the rivers to a large sawmill at Kilmorack Falls on the River Beauly and until 1947 the birch trees were cut for manufacturing into bobbins for the Indian jute mills, an industry that came to an end when India became independent. The Forestry Commission took over the glen in

Top: Loch Affric   Above: Glen Affric

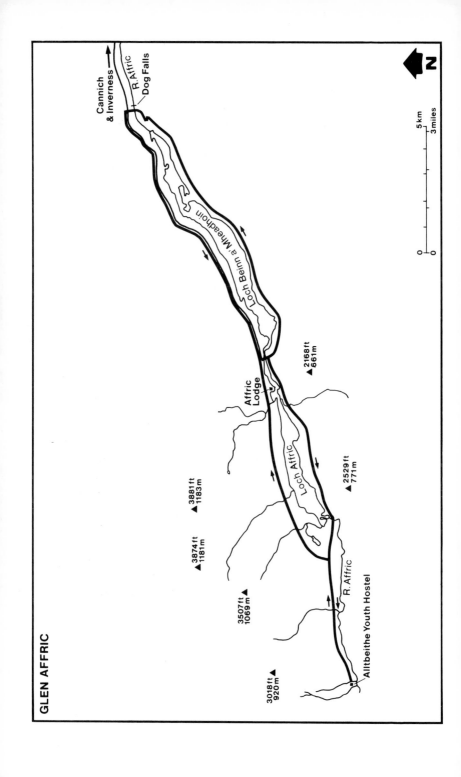

GLEN AFFRIC

1951, fenced in the native forest and killed all the deer within the enclosure in order to allow the forest to regenerate. They also planted some pines from native seed 'in a natural manner'. Without doubt this has removed all sense of wildness and discovery from the glen, but great beauties still remain and the free-standing Scots pines around the loch are a particularly splendid sight.

Map: OS Landranger no. 25

Distance: 31 miles, 50 kilometres

Difficulty: moderate

Time: as logged two days − see route description

Logistics: By car, take the A831 and turn off at Cannich. The nearest train station is at Inverness.

Route description
25.45 miles (40.89km) track/trail, 5.5 miles (8.9km) tarmac.

This is a classic tour for Everyman: the tracks and trails are excellent and nothing is too demanding. A lovely day's ride is to park at the upper car park (mile 6.55) and circle Loch Affric − eleven miles (17.70km) in total. Our tour however, covers a leisurely two days, stopping overnight at Alltbeithe, the most remote Youth Hostel in Britain (don't forget to take a candle). The hostel is an excellent place to use as a base if you are thinking of exploring the area more thoroughly. There are several Munros to climb and a couple of trails to ride, although these are more challenging than the ones around Loch Affric − be prepared to carry.

If you want blasted heaths, dramatic heights or death-defying descents then this is not the tour for you. But for some magnificent scenery, the cream of Scotland's ancient Caledonian Forest, and track which allows you to raise your eyes to enjoy it all, then this one is perfect. Owing to the accessibility of this glen to the motorist, tourists abound at weekends and holiday time (mainly July and August). It is therefore much better to make a visit midweek if possible.

Route Log

00.00m (00.00km) Dog Falls, bridge and car park. Turn left out of the car park onto tarmac.

00.87 (01.39) Hydro Electric dam.

03.25 (05.22) Loch Benevan car park and picnic site.

05.50 (08.84) Bridge, end of tarmac.

06.55 (10.53) Car park and viewpoint, information maps, forest walks, picnic tables. Fork left.

06.66 (10.71) Bridge and locked gate − the small side gate is unlocked.

06.78 (10.90) Fork, go right.

07.58 (12.19) Gate, Glen Affric Lodge on the right.

11.00 (17.69) Gate and fork − go right towards the steadings.

11.37 (18.29) Either ford the river on the right or the burn on the left and then through the steadings to the footbridge.

11.46 (18.43) Cross the footbridge and turn left.

11.86 (19.00) Track from the north side of the loch joins here.

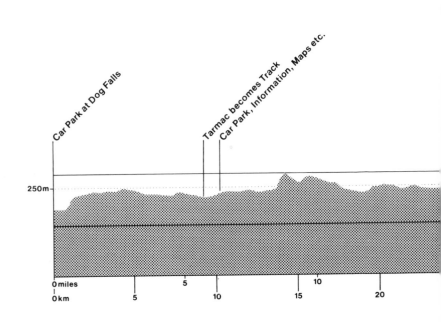

15.00 (24.13) Youth Hostel — Alltbeithe, grade three. No electricity so bring a candle or torch with you. The warden will be able to tell you what state the other trails are in if you are thinking of staying to explore. Backtrack 3.20 miles to the fork.

18.20 (29.28) Fork, for the north trail turn left.

22.63 (36.41) Trail ends, turn left at the lodge gates back onto the track.

23.60 (38.00) Car park, veer right, recross the bridge and through the gate to the fork.

23.84 (38.35) Turn left.

28.30 (45.53) Fork left.

29.40 (47.30) Start ascent.

30.00 (48.27) Summit — start of fun descent (watch out for walkers).

30.36 (48.84) Fork left (if in control).

30.95 (49.79) Dog Falls, bridge and car park.

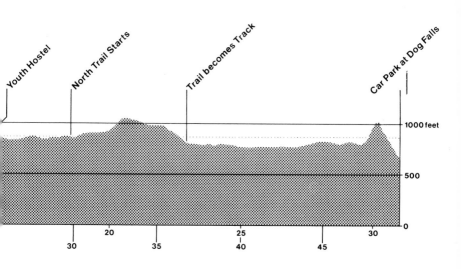

10

Corgarff Castle – Tomintoul

Area information

Corgarff Castle is a sixteenth century tower house which has played an eventful role in Scottish affairs. In 1571 the castle, then in possession of the Forbes' family, was besieged by supporters of the deposed Mary Queen of Scots. When the laird's wife refused to surrender, it was set on fire, killing her with her family and servants. In the early eighteenth century the rebuilt castle was owned by the Earl of Mar and was used by the Jacobites in both the 1715 and 1745 uprisings. It was then converted into barracks for Hanoverian troops and was used in a campaign against smuggling between 1827 and 1831, before slowly falling into disrepair. The castle is now in the care of Historic Buildings and Monuments.

This route takes you through the heather-clad Grampian hills which carry large stocks of Red Grouse. These hills are managed by carefully controlled burning of the heather to increase the number of grouse that live on them. This system of burning the older heather ensures new growth in the variety of stages that the birds need: mature vegetation for cover, young shoots for food and clearings where chicks can sun themselves. They may well explode into chattering flight almost beneath your wheels. Grouse are easily recognisable by their dark colour, plump shape and the male's 'go-back, go-back' alarm call. The grouse shooting season starts on August the twelfth and continues through September.

At Inchrory Lodge the route turns north up Glen Avon to Tomintoul, one of the highest villages in Scotland at 1,132ft (345 metres). There are all services here – the tourist information office, museum, post office and bank are all in the square in the centre of the village. The museum is housed in a former baker's premises and was awarded a special commendation in 1986. Well worth a visit. At mile sixteen is the disused Lecht mine. Between 1730 and 1737 iron ore was mined in the nearby hills; the ore was then taken by packhorse over the hill to Nethy Bridge where there was a plentiful supply of wood for smelting. Later, in 1841, the

Looking towards Corgarff Castle

mine was reopened to produce manganese ore. A crushing plant driven by a water wheel was installed – the building that housed it can be seen from the picnic site. This time the ore was taken to Portgordon on the Moray coast from where it was shipped to Newcastle for use in the manufacture of bleach. Although at first successful, it was closed down in 1846 due to a fall in the price of ore. In winter the summit of the Lecht pass is a busy ski area, with both downhill and cross country.

Map: OS Landranger nos. 36 and 37
Distance: 23 miles, 37 kilometres
Difficulty: easy
Time: half a day
Logistics: by road, the A939 Tomintoul-Cockbridge.

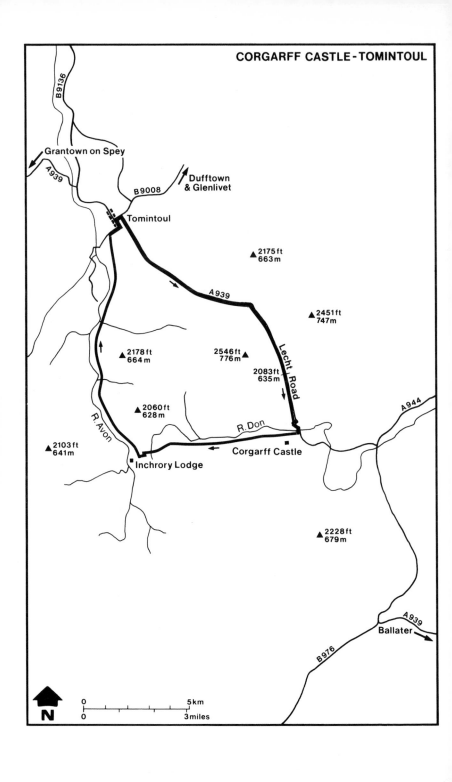

Route description
6.92 miles (10.97km) of track and 16 miles (25.93km) of tarmac.

I started this tour at Corgarff Castle because I enjoyed finishing at 45 mph down the Lecht. If, on the other hand, you prefer to finish with a hot cup of tea or a cold pint awaiting you, start and finish at Tomintoul.

The log starts at the dour and solitary Corgarff Castle. From the castle car park the route heads west on tarmac for one and three-quarter miles. A track then takes you onto the heatherclad moorland, home to the famous Red Grouse. If the thought of these birds being shot offends your sensibilities, it would be unwise to ride this route on August the twelfth when the grouse shooting season opens. The best time to do this tour is July or August when the heather is in bloom. The track climbs to 1,608 feet (490m) before descending to Inchrory Lodge. This is a fun descent, with some good corners to catch one out. Turning right at Inchrory (a shooting lodge which looks curiously out of place in this secret glen), the track soon turns to tarmac. This part of the glen is rather bleak. The unfortunate rabbit population is prone to myxamatosis − a deadly disease (which was introduced into Europe by a Frenchman) which strikes in epidemic proportions and leads to a slow and painful death. There are fossils to be found in the sedimentary rocks here. Some very pretty woods at the north end of the glen provide relief from the previous barrenness, and at mile eleven a nature trail leaves the tarmac for a mile and a half. An easy track with a short steep ascent peaking at Queen Victoria's viewpoint brings one into the village of Tomintoul. In the town square there is a very helpful tourist information office with an interesting museum connected. Mountain bikes can be hired at the hotel (see p.106 for mountain bike hire list) but it is wise to call ahead to check availability. There is also a Youth Hostel, along with a bank, post office, and shops. The last section of this tour (all tarmac) is the perfect example of both the agony and the ecstasy of bicycling. There is a long, steep (20% gradient) climb to the summit of the Lecht − 2,083 feet (635m), followed by a screaming downhill. Check all systems before taking off for these two miles of teary-eyed, downhill bliss. An excellent finish to any ride.

Route Log

00.00m (00.00km) Corgarff Castle car park.

00.49 (00.79) Locked gate.

01.85 (02.98) Tarmac ends.

02.21 (03.56) Gate.

02.51 (04.04) Fork, turn right. Grouse beaters' bothy on the right, the left track goes to a small loch with a dam.

02.99 (04.80) Fork, keep straight.

04.75 (07.65) T-junction turn right.

05.02 (08.08) Keeper's house.

05.45 (08.77) Inchrory Lodge, turn right.

07.29 (11.74) Tarmac.

09.98 (16.07) Fork, keep straight. Bridge over the river Avon on the left.

10.44 (16.80) Through farmyard.

11.03 (17.76) Fork, turn right onto track — signposted country walk.

12.06 (19.42) Gate — short walk to Queen Victoria's viewpoint.

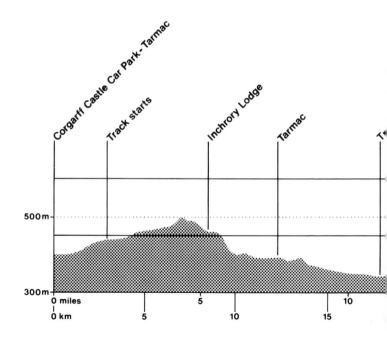

12.41 (20.00) Join tarmac, keep straight.

13.00 (20.93) Tomintoul, turn left for the town centre and services.

13.28 (21.38) Town square − tourist information, museum, mountain bike hire, restaurant. Backtrack and turn left on A939.

13.35 (21.50) Turn left, A939.

13.60 (21.90) Turn right − Lecht road to Cockbridge.

15.42 (24.83) Restaurant/tearoom, whisky and gift shop.

16.35 (26.33) Picnic site, disused mine, good camping place on the left. Start ascent.

20.07 (32.32) Lecht ski centre, telephone, cafe (only open in winter).

20.76 (33.44) Summit.

22.60 (36.40) Allargue Inn on the right.

22.74 (36.62) End of descent, right turn to car park.

22.92 (36.90) Car park.

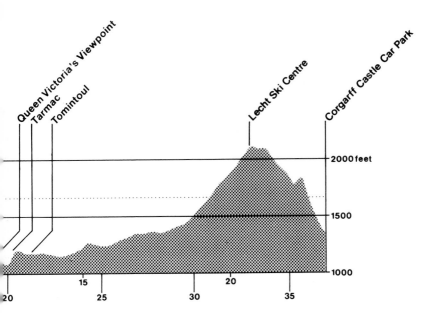

Typical Speyside track

11

Speyside

Area information
The tour starts from Elgin, the principal town of Morayshire. The name is supposed to be derived from Helgy, a general of the army of Sigurd, the Norwegian Earl of Orkney who conquered Caithness, Ross, Sutherland and Moray around 927AD. The surrounding area was a favourite hunting ground of the early Scottish monarchs. David I raised Elgin to the status of a royal burgh and in 1224 the town received the additional accolade of being chosen as the seat of the Bishop of Moray. Elgin cathedral must have been, when entire, a glorious building. It is impressive, even in its ruined state. In its original form it was a simple cruciform building but after it was damaged by fire in 1270, a more substantial edifice was built. In 1390 Alexander Stewart, better known as the Wolf of Badenoch, plundered and burned Forres and Elgin, including the cathedral. Once again it was necessary to carry out substantial rebuilding. But sadly it was always to be much too rich a target to last for long. In 1567 the lead was stripped from the roofs and thereafter it gradually collapsed until about 1824 when a Keeper was appointed. From this time onward the conservation of the building became the concern of successive government departments so that the ruins seen today comprise one of the finest examples of mediaeval architecture in Scotland.

Also worth a visit is the Elgin museum which contains a wide range of exhibits illustrating the history of the area, and a unique collection of fossils from 200-400 million years ago. The Thunderton Hotel, just off the High Street, is all that remains of the most splendid house in Elgin which was once a royal residence, with orchards and a bowling green. In mediaeval times it was the site of the 'great lodging' of the Scottish kings and in 1746 Bonnie Prince Charlie stayed here on his way to Culloden.

Elgin is an attractive town: its centre retains some traditional closes and arcaded shops and there are some striking Georgian public buildings. There are all services − hotels, B&B, shops, banks and restaurants. There is a campsite, The Riverside campsite, situated just outside the town on the Inverness road − the A96(T). From the restaurants I visited, I recommend Abbey Court (restaurant only) and Clouseau's (wine bar and restaurant, good selection of malt whiskies). For addresses and telephone numbers see p.88. The extremely friendly and helpful tourist information office is situated at the east end of the High Street (see map).

The River Spey, after which this area is named, is the third largest river in Scotland (after the Tay and the Tweed), with a catchment area of 1,097 square miles (28,424ha.). Many argue that it is the most magnificent of all Scottish rivers, and certainly the view of the upper part of Strathspey looking southwards from near Dulnain bridge towards the Cairngorm mountains is in a league of its own. One of the Spey's unique features is that nowhere, to within half a mile of its mouth, does its current relax. There is no tidal estuary here and in high spate the Spey colours the Moray Firth brown with peat water several miles out to sea. After heavy rainfall the river can rise rapidly, although nothing recently has compared with the great Moray floods of 1829, when, after one night of rain in early August, the Spey rose to around twenty-five feet above its normal level and poured indiscriminately over its banks. Rothes was flooded up to the level of first floor windows and every bridge over the Spey was washed away, except that at Craigellachie which exists to this day.

Another feature of the Spey is the large snow reservoir in which it rises, high up in the Cairngorms. Many miles of its catchment area on the north and west slopes of the Cairngorms are over 3,000 feet (915m) in height and deep snow can last there until as late as June. As it slowly melts, it helps keep the Spey running at a fair height through the spring months, irrespective of the actual rainfall. This is of course crucial to the salmon fisherman in pursuit of his quarry. The runs of salmon in the river, their size and the quality of the fishing are almost legendary. The succession of holding pools together with the flast flow of water and the rocky nature of the river-bed, provide magnificent fishing, particularly with the fly. The season officially opens on February 11th but nowadays it is nearer April or May before the main spring run of fish enters the river.

Speyside's fame lies not only with the fishing fraternity for it is also the very heart of Scotland's malt whisky industry. I refer here to quantity: some would say that the cream of the single malts come from the distilleries on the Island of Islay over on the West Coast. The fact is, however, that there are more distilleries on Speyside per square mile than anywhere else in the world.

The true origin of whisky is shrouded in the mists of time. It is possible that, like Christianity, it came to Scotland from Ireland. It is known to have been the drink of the Highlands for very many centuries, as much for the common man as for clan chieftains and kings. The name whisky is derived from the Gaelic uisgebeatha, commonly shortened to 'usky' in colloquial bar language, which means 'water of life', a definition with which many as well as Scotsmen entirely agree. Distilling whisky is really very simple and requires no elaborate technology or complex machinery. This naturally allowed for a great cottage industry of illegal distillers before a licensing system was introduced (1551 in England, 1755 in Scotland). The tradition of enjoying a dram without troubling the excise man continues to this day, less in Speyside than in Ireland where the illicit whisky called 'poteen' or 'potheen' may even now be found.

Whisky consists of only three ingredients: malted barley, water and yeast. Few distilleries now malt their own barley, the vast majority preferring to buy it pre-malted. Many master distillers will tell you that it is primarily the water that gives each whisky its own unique taste. A common theory is that water running off granite and through peat makes the best whisky. Many a whisky drinker will attribute near magical qualities to the water source used for his or her favourite dram.

There are four basic steps involved in producing a malt whisky. First the barley must be malted. The second step is fermenting an extract of the malt, called wort, with yeast. The alcohol is then collected by evaporation and condensation, a step which is known as distillation. This 'spirit' − legally it cannot be called whisky until it has matured for three years − is about 75% alcohol and is very clear when it leaves the still. It is reduced in strength by adding water. Finally it is poured into oak casks and placed in a bonded warehouse to mature. Whisky acquires its amber colour during maturation, picking it up from the wood of the casks, most of which have been previously used for bourbon or sherry. Matur-

ation can take from five to fifteen years, the quality and price generally increasing with each year in the cask. During this process a small amount of whisky is lost due to evaporation – this is known as the angel's share.

Many of the Speyside distilleries welcome visitors, offering guided tours and often a free dram. Since whisky is made the same way at all the distilleries, the tours tend to be rather similar and either begin or end with a video presentation describing whisky in general and their distillery in particular. These lean more towards advertising than education and become boring very quickly. A tour of the actual distillery follows, including mash house, wash backs, stills and the duty-free house. Finally a free dram is provided. Most of the distilleries that offer tours also have a shop where you can purchase their whisky as well as whisky-related souvenirs. Some distilleries provide a tearoom – to give relief to those for whom the amber-coloured 'water of life' means a good cup of tea. If you plan to include only one distillery in your itinerary, Glenfiddich would be a good choice. The video presentation is impressive, the tour complete, and it is the only distillery on Speyside that bottles the mature whisky at the distillery. On the other hand Cardhu is smaller and more interesting. The following is a list of distilleries welcoming visitors at the time of publication. Some of the distilleries not advertising tours will provide one if you call ahead and ask. It is better to check opening times before riding too far out of your way, as a closed distillery at the top of a hill (Cardhu) is somewhat frustrating. Also remember that the drink driving laws apply to bicyclists as well as to car drivers – know your limit!

Distilleries offering tours are:

Glen Grant, Rothes. Tours and tasting from May to October, Monday to Friday, 10.00 am-4.00 pm. Reception centre and shop. Tel. 03403-413.

The Macallan, Craigellachie. Tours by arrangement only. Tel. 03405-471.

Aberlour, Charlestown of Aberlour. Tours morning only 9.00 am-11.00 am, Monday to Friday. Tel. 03405-204.

Tamdhu, Speyside. Tours and tasting from Easter to the end of May, open Monday to Friday: from June to end of September, open Monday to Saturday, 10.00 am-4.00 pm. Small shop. Tel. 03406-221.

Cardhu, Upper Knockando. Tours and tasting, open all year Monday to Friday, from May to September Saturdays also, 9.30 am-4.30 pm. Evening tours on request. Large shop, an excellent tearoom, interesting tour. Tel. 03406-204.

Cragganmore, Bridge of Avon. Tours by arrangement only. Tel. 08072-202.

Glenfarclas, Ballindalloch. Tours and tasting, open all year, Monday to Friday 9.00 am-4.30 pm. From June to September, Saturdays also − 10.00 am-4.00 pm. Good tour, excellent shop. Tel. 08072-257.

The Glenlivet, Tomintoul. Tours and tasting, open April to October, Monday to Saturday, 10.00 am-4.00 pm. Expensive shop, good tearoom. Tel. 08073-427.

Tomnavulin-Glenlivet, Tomintoul. Tours and tasting, open spring to October, 10.00 am-4.00 pm daily except Sunday. Shop. Tel. 08073-442.

Glenfiddich, Dufftown. Tours and tasting, open all year Monday to Friday, 9.30 am-4.30 pm; Easter to mid-October open on Saturday and Sunday 12.00 noon-4.30 pm. Good tours (includes bottling) and shop. Tel. 0340-20373.

Campsites
Riverside caravan park, West Road, Elgin. Tel. 0343-2813.
Aberlour Gardens caravan park, Charlestown of Aberlour. Tel. 03405-586.
Fochabers Burnside caravan park, Fochabers. Tel. 0343-820362.
Boat O' Fiddich campsite (no services). Speyside.

Restaurants
From the restaurants I visited, I can recommend the following:

Abbey Court Restaurant, 15 Greyfriars Street, Elgin. Tel. 0343-542849.

Clouseau's Wine Bar and Restaurant, Red Lion Close, 48 High Street, Elgin. Tel. 0343-549737 (also has a good selection of malt whiskies).

Ed's Cafe, Main Street, Rothes. Good, cheap food, large servings — excellent record selection on the juke box.

The Old Pantry Tearoom, The Square, Aberlour (delicious bacon and melted cheese rolls).

Blairfindy Lodge Hotel, Glenlivet, Ballindalloch, Banffshire. Tel. 08073-376. (I did not eat in the restaurant but the bar food was excellent.)

Taste of Speyside, 10 Balvenie Street, Dufftown, Banffshire. Tel. 0340-20860 — a good selection of malts, good food at reasonable prices, open for just tea or coffee. If you want dinner it is wise to book.

Gordon Arms Hotel, Fochabers, Moray. Tel. 0343-820508 — a good selection of malt whiskies and very good bar food (the restaurant menu was imaginative and sounded delicious).

Speybay Hotel, Speybay. Good bar food and Motown music.

If you have space in your panniers and are intending to do some shopping, then for an outstanding choice of woollens and cashmere you can do no better than Johnston's of Elgin, Newmill, Elgin. There are tours of the mill Monday to Thursday if you make an appointment. Tel. 0343-547821.

Cycle and mountain bike hire in the area:

Flycycle Holidays, 8 The Square, Cullen. Tel. 0542-40638.

I. J. Williamson, 7 High Street, Elgin. Tel. 0343-549656.

Findhorn Bay Bikes, The Apothecary, Findhorn Bay Caravan Park, Findhorn. Tel. 0309-31044.

The Gallery, 85 High Street, Fochabers. Tel. 0343-820981; and The Old School, 31 Bogmoor, Speybay. Tel. 0343-821432. Helmets also for hire; delivery and collection of bikes can be arranged.

McLeans, Gordon Street, Forres. Tel. 0343-73028.

Denis Shepherd, 12 Moss Street, Keith. Tel. 05422-7934.

Hillcraft, 73 Main Street, Tomintoul. Tel. 09752-207.

Prices for hiring bikes seem to differ enormously from firm to firm. It is always wise in any case to check that they hire the quality of bike you prefer before turning up on their doorstep.

SPEYSIDE

Spey Bay
Bogmoor
B9104
Fochabers
Garmouth
R. Spey
Boat o' Brig
B9015
A96(T)
1545ft
471m
Lhanbryde
B9103
Auchinroath
B9015
Rothes
Elgin
A941
Green Hill
1102ft/336m
Thomshill
Red Taingy
1096ft/334m

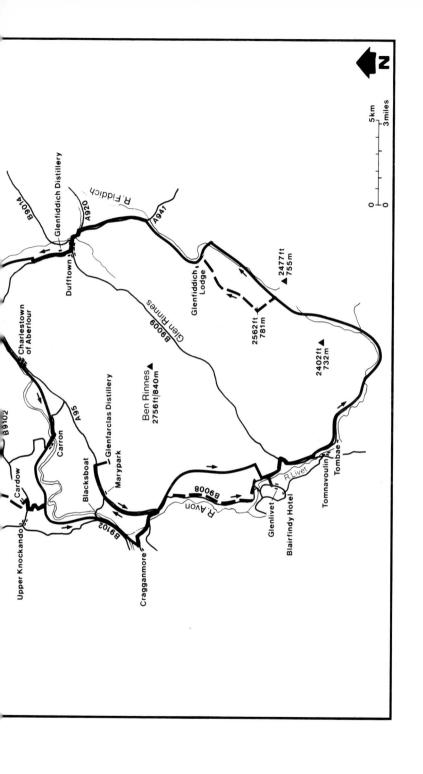

Map: OS Landranger nos. 28, 36, 37

Distance: 86 miles, 138 kilometres

Difficulty: easy

Time: three days minimum; we suggest at least a week

Logistics: Train to Elgin. Main road routes are: A96(T) Aberdeen, A941 Dufftown, A95 Grantown.

Route description

If you like malt whisky, then this is the tour for you! I have tried to design a loop which includes a variety of distilleries, riding on the Speyside Way and on some mountain track/trail.

The tour starts from Elgin and almost immediately there is a choice between a tarmac section or hill route. The hill route has a short but nasty stretch at the summit where the trail disappears into peat bogs, not too bad if the weather has been dry but expect to get wet feet otherwise. At Craigellachie the route joins the Speyside Way until it reaches Cragganmore — approximately 8 miles. (The Speyside Way is a long distance footpath from the Cairngorms to the sea, following the Spey Valley). The logged route follows footpaths, minor roads and disused railways lines. There is a visitor centre near Craigellachie at Boat O' Fiddich (mile 58.50 in log). The spur to Tomintoul runs over the hills of Avonside, making use of historic drove and cart roads. The character of the route changes dramatically here and becomes much tougher. I have offered an alternative route here — mile 29 of the log. The mountain route is excellent, a tough mixture of track and trail through the heather but there are many stiles, and *a lot* of lifting which can be exhausting with panniers. The route is now in Glenlivet country, a name familiar to all malt whisky drinkers. Such is the fame of this glen that many distillers outwith the glen itself add the word Glenlivet as a suffix to the name of their own products, though only one distillery has the right to use the name on its own. From here the route becomes track for nine and a half miles (15.28km) through the beautiful and remote Glenfiddich, after which you join the A941 to Dufftown (all services). Rejoining the Speyside Way, a mixture of track and tarmac brings you to Speybay, the northernmost point of the long distance path and where the River Spey joins the open sea. At Tugnet there is a permanent exhibition of the history of the fishing in the area, situated in the old ice house and well worth a visit. The Speyside Way is well signposted and there are information maps, picnic tables and benches at regular intervals. In general this is a relaxing tour geared to experiencing the area rather than serious mountain biking. Speyside has much to offer and you should allow plenty of time for this one.

Speyside stile

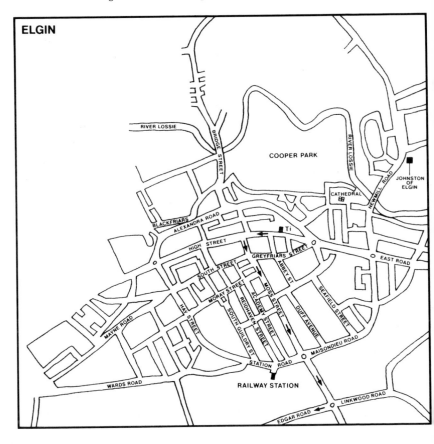

Route Log

00.00m (00.00km) Elgin, tourist information office, head for second roundabout (see map).

00.70 (01.13) Roundabout, go west on Edgar Road.

01.11 (01.79) Turn left, Glen Moray Drive, housing estate.

01.37 (02.21) Turn left then right onto Sandy Road.

01.64 (02.64) Turn right.

02.71 (04.36) Fork, straight on.

03.62 (05.83) Fork, straight on.

04.10 (06.60) Glenlossie Distillery and Manochmore Distillery. No tours.

04.50 (07.25) Turn left, opposite Birnie Inn, or take optional hill route.

Hill Route

This starts with a constant moderate uphill on a good track and finishes with a long constant downhill on track, but the half-mile section on the summit crosses an unrideable peat bog as the track disappears. This route is a fair-weather route and is not advised when the ground is very wet. The log is as follows:

00.00m (00.00km) Start route.
01.00 (01.61) Fork left.
01.75 (02.82) Track, start ascent.
02.90 (04.67) Fork, take left track.
03.40 (05.48) Summit.
04.71 (07.58) Fork, take right track.
04.98 (08.00) Fork, take left track − very faint, easily missed.
05.20 (08.37) Fork, take left trail where track turns sharply uphill.
05.35-05.85 (08.61-09.42) Trail disappears, cross the bog staying near the fence.
06.00 (09.66) Start descent.
07.00 (11.27) Forestry track on the right − stay straight.
08.27 (13.32) Cross tarmac, continue on track.
08.83 (14.22) Fork, take left track.
08.93 (14.38) Turn left on tarmac to distillery.
09.18 (14.78) Cardhu distillery. To rejoin Speyside Way from Cardhu, turn right on B9102 and follow signs to Tamdhu distillery. (See mile 22.76 in log.)

Return to main log

04.85 (07.80) Moray Stone Cutters − a fascinating place.
05.06 (08.15) Turn right at crossroads onto track.
05.77 (09.29) Cross tarmac, continue up track and through the wood.
06.14 (09.89) Straight on, track deteriorates.
06.28 (10.11) Tarmac, turn right on the old road.
06.40 (10.30) Turn right onto A941.
06.75 (10.87) Coleburn distillery on the left − no tours.
08.47 (13.64) Rothes Glen Hotel − three star, BTA recommended hotel and restaurant.
09.35 (15.05) Turn left − signposted Auchinroath.
10.83 (17.44) Speyburn distillery − no tours.

The Square, Aberlour

11.14 (17.94) T-junction, turn right on B9015.

11.41 (18.37) Road joins and becomes A941. Glen Grant distillery − open to the public (see p.87).

11.78 (19.00) Glen Spey distillery (no tours) and Rothes Castle ruin on the right.

11.86 (19.10) Ed's Cafe on the left (see p.88).

11.97 (19.27) Turn left at the end of town.

12.08 (19.45) Turn right onto railway.

12.63 (20.34) Turn right.

12.66 (20.39) Turn left onto road − A941.

13.88 (22.35) Keep straight. (B9102 joins here).

14.32 (23.06) Tourist information map on the right, turn right over Telford's bridge.

14.43 (23.24) Bridge.

14.60 (23.51) Turn left on A941.

14.65 (23.60) Turn right into Craigellachie − post office, hotels, shop, telephone.

14.79 (23.82) Glen Avon hotel, turn left down driveway to the Speyside Way.

14.84 (23.90) Steps and ramp down to railway, turn left at the bottom.

15.68 (25.25) Left turn to camping ground, half a mile up the hill, walled garden, hot showers, limited shop.

16.37 (26.36) Walkers Shortbread factory. Considered by many to be the best shortbread made in Scotland; no tours but a mouthwatering shop full of free samples. They will post gifts if required.

16.75 (27.00) Left turn to the centre of Aberlour. There is an excellent cafe in the square, The Old Pantry (eating too much shortbread is thirsty work). Aberlour distillery is at the end of the town on the left − open to the public in the morning (see page 87). Backtrack to Speyside Way.

17.02 (27.40) T-junction on path, turn left. Very pretty bridge across the Spey on the right.

17.07 (27.48) Turn right, back onto the railway.

18.93 (30.50) Fork, keep straight, distillery warehouse on the right.

19.24 (30.98) Crossroads of tracks, keep straight. Daluaine Halt, deer farm, and distillery (no tours) on the left.

19.90 (32.00) Cross the road.

19.98 (32.17) Carron Bridge over the Spey.

20.08 (32.33) Turn left through the fence.

20.26 (32.62) Carron village, information map, pub, post box. Turn left then right by the distillery (no tours).

20.40 (32.85) Bear left off the tarmac onto the railway.

22.49 (36.22) Knockando distillery (no tours, owned by J&B).

22.76 (36.65) Tamdhu distillery − open to the public (see p.87). Alternative hill route from Elgin connects here. Three mile round side trip from Tamdhu to Cardhu distillery. Cardhu has an excellent tearoom and shop and gives one of the more interesting tours. On the way there or on your return stop at Knockando Woollen Mill (signposted) and step back in time, a magic place selling beautiful tweed and wool rugs at extremely reasonable prices. It is one of the few woollen mills left that has its own teasel machine − ask to see the workshop.

Continue along the railway.

25.00 (40.25) Blacksboat railway station, information map, picnic tables − no services.

26.63 (42.88) Bridge over the Spey.

26.77 (43.10) Tarmac, turn left. End of maintained railway track. A quarter of a mile to the right is Cragganmore distillery − tours by appointment only.

27.63 (44.49) Turn left onto A95.

27.85 (44.85) Standing stones on the right.

28.08 (45.22) River Avon bridge and old bridge. Ballindalloch lodge and the entrance to Ballindalloch castle which is only open on Sundays − 10.00 am-2.00 pm. Shop and post office.

28.43 (45.78) Turn right onto the B9008. For a side tour of Glenfarclas distillery, keep left on the A95 and at 03.10 miles (4.98km) turn right at the distillery sign. The distillery is a quarter of a mile down the drive. Although everybody has their own preferred dram, this whisky reasily ranks with the best and is worth a tasting (see page 88). There is an excellent shop. Backtrack to junction.

29.00 (46.70) Turn left to Auldich Farm for mountain route − good but many stiles you have to lift the bike over. The alternative tarmac route for the fainthearted (or sensible): 4.38 miles (7.04km) long, very friendly tearoom and B&B at mile 01.63 (02.62) (The Old Manse), at 02.50 (04.02) junction B9136 turn left. At 03.18 (05.11) Bridge of Livet, wool shop, post office. At mile 04.38 (07.04) rejoin main route.

Daluaine Distillery

29.28 (47.15) Auldich Farm. B&B.

29.63 (47.71) Car Park, information map. Tarmac ends soon after.

30.17 (45.58) Leave track, fork right. Trail deteriorates badly.

31.13 (50.13) Turn right.

31.19 (50.23) Summit. Post, turn left and follow the fence.

31.27 (50.35) Turn right.

32.14 (51.75) Turn left over the fence, across stile and follow the fence.

32.53 (52.38) Stile − cross and turn left onto the trail between two fences.

32.63 (52.54) Turn right − three stiles.

32.86 (52.91) Turn left − two stiles.

32.90 (52.98) Cross stile onto track, turn left.

32.94 (53.00) Farm, bear right downhill − becomes tarmac.

33.25 (53.54) Junction with B9008, telephone box, public hall. Turn left.

33.57 (54.00) Turn right off road for detour to Glenlivet distillery food and pub.

Tamdhu

00.10 (00.16) Footbridge over the River Livet.

00.57 (00.92) T-junction, turn left on singletrack road.

00.69 (01.10) Glenlivet distillery (open to public − see p.88). Half a mile further up the hill on the right is the Blairfindy Lodge Hotel, smart but bicycle friendly and good bar food. Backtrack to B9008.

34.30 (55.23) Junction, stay right on B9008. Post box.

35.57 (57.28) Turn left on tarmac, signposted to Tombae.

36.15 (58.21) Footpath on the right to Tomnavulin-Glenlivet distillery. Half a mile round trip detour − distillery open to the public (see page 88). Tearoom in Tomnavulin village.

36.43 (58.66) Church and track on the left, stay right on the tarmac.

37.89 (61.00) Memorial, tarmac ends, take the right hand track.

38.00 (61.20) Trail goes right towards footbridge − signposted Glenlivet estate.

38.19 (61.50) Do not cross the footbridge, follow the trail up the burn. Several gates in the next mile.

38.87 (62.59) Gate, turn right on the track.

38.99 (62.78) Footbridge or ford.

40.89 (65.85) Ford, immediately after turn left.

41.36 (66.60) Abandoned lodge.

41.59 (66.97) Fork, take left track.

42.79 (68.90) Ford burn, start ascent.

43.56 (70.14) Cairn − V.R. 1867 carved on the stone.

43.71 (70.38) Fork go right. Alternative steep and very rugged route to the left.

43.79 (70.51) Summit.

44.99 (72.45) Private bothy.

45.44 (73.17) Ford.

47.14 (75.90) T-junction, turn left.

47.43 (76.38) Sawmill, tarmac begins.

47.74 (76.88) Alternative route rejoins here.

47.99 (77.28) Glenfiddich Lodge, fork − stay right.

50.45 (81.24) Locked gate, footgate on the right. Junction A941, turn left.

52.92 (85.22) T-junction, turn left on A941 towards Dufftown.

53.34 (85.90) T-junction, turn left keeping on A941.

53.80 (86.63) Dufftown square. Tourist information, turn right (A941) − restaurant, cafe (The Taste of Speyside), post office, good second hand bookshop.

54.39 (87.58) Glenfiddich distillery, open to the public (see page 88).

54.84 (88.31) Turn right onto Speyside Way. Car park, picnic site, information map.

54.96 (88.50) Convalmore distillery (no tours).

58.50 (94.20) Crossroads at Boat O' Fiddich. Lovely campsite by the river and visitors centre − no showers or shop at time of writing. Picnic site, information map. Turn right and right again on the tarmac. Cross bridge.

58.56 (94.30) Turn left at Fiddichside Inn (delightful pub, no food) and head up the hill.

61.18 (98.52) Fork right onto track, start long ascent.

61.90 (99.68) Take left track.

62.24 (100.22) Fine viewpoint on the left.

62.40 (100.48) Summit.

63.60 (102.42) Fork left down the path.

64.75 (104.27) Fork left near interesting sign − KEEP LOW, FULL BORES AND BULLETS OVERHEAD.

64.79 (104.33) Keep straight.

Disused railway on Speyside Way

64.89 (104.50) Turn left.

65.21 (105.00) Turn right and then bear left towards river.

65.57 (105.59) Turn left.

65.62 (105.67) Turn right on path.

65.65 (105.72) Turn right on tarmac then left under railway bridge, start steep ascent.

66.13 (106.50) Summit.

66.95 (107.80) Keep straight.

68.67 (110.58) Sharp descent followed by steep uphill.

69.20 (111.43) Summit, picnic site − tables.

70.12 (112.91) Turn left.

70.14 (112.95) Turn right, narrow path.

70.52 (113.56) Crossroads, straight over.

70.72 (113.88) Tarmac, straight on.

70.80 (114.00) Turn right then left.

70.91 (114.20) Cross the street. Turn right here for detour into Fochabers − brilliant museum, Gordon Arms Hotel for good bar food and mouthwatering but expensive dining room menu. Campground with hot showers next to Garden Centre and tearoom.

71.05 (114.40) Bear right.

71.10 (114.49) Bear left.

71.44 (115.00) Turn right after two bridges.

71.53 (115.18) Turn left onto tarmac road B9104.

72.08 (116.00) Turn left onto river path.

72.43 (116.63) Fork, take left track.

72.56 (116.84) Fork, keep straight.

72.88 (117.36) Fork, keep straight.

73.95 (119.08) Fork turn right.

74.03 (119.21) Fork, turn right.

74.36 (119.74) Fork left.

74.96 (120.70) Dismantled railway bridge, straight on for a two mile round trip to Speybay. Excellent museum, hotel − bar food, campsite. Turn left.

75.13 (120.98) Speybridge.

75.79 (122.04) Tarmac, turn left. Telephone.

75.91 (122.24) Turn left.

79.11 (127.40) Crossroads, straight over.

80.30 (129.30) T-junction, A96(T). Turn right.

80.36 (129.40) Turn left to Fogwatt and Millbuies.

Spey Bridge

81.11 (130.61) Turn left then right.
81.92 (131.91) Turn right − unsigned.
83.76 (134.88) Linkwood distillery (no tours). Continue on this road.
84.69 (136.38) Roundabout, turn right.
84.86 (136.53) Roundabout, turn left for railway station, straight on for tourist information office.
85.50 (137.68) Tourist information office, Elgin.

Tourist Information Centres and British Rail

Tourist information centres

Aviemore 0479-810363
Ballachulish* 08552-296
Ballater* 03397-55306
Banchory* 03302-2000
Braemar* 03383-600
Broadford* 04712-361
Carr Bridge* 047984-634
Dufftown* 0340-20501
Edinburgh 031-557-1700
Elgin 0343-2666
Fochabers* 0343-820770
Fort William and
  Lochaber 0397-3781

Glasgow 041-227-4878
Grantown on Spey* 0479-2773
Inveraray* 0499-2063
Inverness 0463-234353
Killin* 05672-254
Kingussie* 05402-297
Kyle of Lochalsh* 0599-4276
Lochcarron* 05202-354
Mallaig* 0687-2170
Skye, Isle of, and
  Wester Ross 0478-2137
Tomintoul* 08074-285

* denotes offices which are closed in winter (effectively, mid-October to Easter).

British Rail Stations

Elgin 0343-3407
Edinburgh 031-556-2451
Fort William 0397-3791

Glasgow 041-204-2844
Oban 0631-63083

Bike Parts and Suppliers, Bike Hire

This list does not cover all shops and hire in Scotland. It is intended only as a guide to parts stockists, repairs and hire in the general area of the tours. For additional information please contact the Scottish Tourist Board which is very helpful (see previous page). The shops marked with an asterisk (*) hold a good range of Shimano parts but if even these prove unsatisfactory then Madison (Newcastle), telephone 091-261-9995, will post direct to you.

Aberdeen
Cycling World, 460 George Street. 0224-632994*

Aviemore
Ellisbrigham. 0479-810175
Speyside Sports. 0497-810656
Sporthouse. 0479-810655
Sportshire, Nethybridge. 0479-82333
Slochd Ski Sport, Carrbridge. 0479-84666
Inverdruie, Rothiemurchus. 0479-810787

Buckie
Horizon Cycle Hire. 0542-33070

Dufftown
I. & H. Massie, 5 Fife Street. 0340-20559/20906

Dundee
Nicholson, 2 Forfar Road. 0382-461212*

Edinburgh
Edinburgh Bicycle Co-Op, 8 Alvanley Terrace, Whitehouse Lane. 031-228-1368*
Robin Williamson, 26 Hamilton Place, Stockbridge. 031-225-3286*

Fort William
Off-Beat Bikes (Dave Austen). 0397-702663
Lees Cycle Hire. 0397-704204

Glasgow
Dales, 150 Dobbies Loan. 041-332-2705*

Glencoe
Glencoe Bike Hire (Steve or Nancy Kennedy). 08552-685

Glenfinnan
Clark, Craiglea, Lochailort. 06877-273

Inverness
Thorntons, 23 Castle Street. Shop: 0463-222810; Workshop: 0463-235078*
Highland Cycles, 26 Greig Street. 0463-710462*

Kinlochleven
Leven Cycles. 21-22 Leven Road. 08554-614*

Oban
The Cycle Shop, Tregard Road. Hire & repair. 0631-66996

Tomintoul
Bridge of Brown Tea Room. 08074-335

Restaurants

Finding good home cooking at a reasonable price can be difficult in Scotland. When in doubt, it is usually more rewarding to go vegetarian. The following suggestions either always have a selection of vegetarian meals or will cook to order.

Name	Town	Tel. No.
Osprey Hotel	Kingussie	0540-661510
Culloden Pottery	Inverness	0667-462749
Culloden House	Inverness	0463-790461
Brookes Wine Bar	Inverness	0463-225662
Highland Designworks	Kyle of Lochalsh	0599-4388
Braeval Old Mill	Aberfoyle	08772-711
Cuilfail Hotel	Kilmelford	08522-274
The Lorne Pub	Oban	0631-66766
The Oban Inn	Oban	0631-62484
Littlejohns	Perth Stirling	0738-39888 0786-63222
Green House	Struan, Isle of Skye	047072-293
Three Chimneys	Colbost, Dunvegan Isle of Skye	047082-258
Three Rowans	Edinbane, Kildonan Isle of Skye	047082-286
Cruachan House, Dinner and/or B&B	Dalmally near Oban	08382-496
Inchbae Lodge Hotel	Garve	09975-269

Bothy accommodation

Bothy	OS Map no.	Map Ref.	Estate	Tel. no.
Culra	41 & 42	523763	Ben Alder	05282-224
Blackburn of Pattack	41 & 42	544817	Ardverikie	05283-200
Lairigleach (Corrour-Spean Bridge)	41	282736	British Aluminium Co.	0397-2411
Meanach (Luibeilt)	41	266685	British Aluminium Co.	08554-337
Camban	26	053184	Glen Affric	04565-288
Staoineag	41	296679	None	None

Glossary of Scottish words used in this book

Bealloch: a small saddle between two higher parts of a hill.

Bothy: a single-storied building traditionally used to house unmarried seasonal labourers.

Brae: a steep slope.

Burn: a stream.

Cairn: a man-made pile of stones, usually conical.

Croft: a smallholding.

Drover: one who drove livestock to market, often over very long distances.

Factor: the agent of a landlord.

Fank: a pen, or system of pens, used for handling sheep.

Forest (as in deer forest): an estate used for deer-stalking. The only trees found in these forests are usually modern plantations.

Kirk: church.

Laird: landed proprietor; sometimes used sarcastically, in the same way as *sahib*.

Lodge: where the laird of a forest occasionally resides.

Marching (with): of estates, sharing a common boundary.

Munro: a hill over 3,000 feet (915m) in height.

Outwith: outside, not near, more distant (also in relation to time).

Policy: usually in the plural, the pleasure grounds of a mansion.

Pursy: of people, short-breathed and fat; of horses, broken-winded.

Spate: a flood in a burn or river.

Steadings: farm buildings.

Strath: a valley of considerable extent, larger than a glen and usually fertile.

NOTES

NOTES

NOTES

NOTES

NOTES

NOTES

NOTES

NOTES

NOTES